There are more things in heaven
and earth, Horatio,
Than are dreamt in your philosophy.
Hamlet
Act 1, Scene 5

NO VACANCY. A sign of the times at Hot Lake Hotel. The hotel, which sits at the base of a hill midway between La Grande and Union, is a haunting sight these days, light years from the time when the railroad stopped every day at its door, bringing affluent visitors from all over the world to sample the healing waters of the "Mayo Clinic of the West". Today there's no vacancy at Hot Lake Hotel--at least for humans. (Rainy Day Press Photo)

NO PARKING!
NO CAMPING!

VIOLATORS WILL BE PROSOCUTED.
VEHICLE WILL BE TOWED AWAY AT
VEHICLE OWNERS EXPENSE

NO
TRESSPASSING!

UNLESS BY PERMISSION OF OWNER OR CARETAKER.
WE WILL NOT TAKE RESPONSABILITY FOR INJURY
TO ANYONE CAUGHT TRESSPASSING

NO
TRESPASSING

WE'RE
SED

GONE HOME. Some do, some don't. A scene from the Jacksonville Cemetery, Jacksonville, Oregon. (Rainy Day Press Photo)

THE CHARLES APPLEGATE HOUSE. This old house, which looks today much less haunted than it did when this photo was taken, was built between 1852 and 1856 by Charles Applegate on his farm near Yoncalla, Oregon. (Photo Courtesy of the Oregon Historical Society)

THE GHOST OF THE LIGHTHOUSE, an oil painting by Tom Allen of Oregon State University, depict-
ing Muriel Trevenard, who, in the story "The Haunted
Light at Newport by the Sea" by Lischen M. Miller,
disappeared in the old lighthouse at Newport. The
painting is owned by Lincoln County Historical Society, Newport, Oregon, and was photographed with
their permission. (Rainy Day Press Photo)

Oregon's GHOSTS & monsters

By Mike Helm

OREGON COUNTRY LIBRARY

Volume 5

Library of Congress Catalog Card Number
81-51427

International Standard Book Number
0-931742-03-X

Published by One Horse Press
P.O. Box 3035
Eugene, Oregon 97403

Printed in Canada

Acknowledgments

Through the four years of my off and on effort to find Oregon's ghosts and monsters I've spoken with dozens of people in dozens of Oregon communities. I accosted them in their homes, in libraries, taverns, grocery stores, chambers of commerce, museums, police stations, newspaper offices, universities and colleges, farms, and other locations and businesses too numerous to mention. Nearly all of the people on whom I descended--camera, tape recorder, questions and all--were friendly, interested, and very helpful. To you, you dozens of helpful Oregonians, my heartfelt thanks.

I am indebted to the staff members of the following institutions and organizations: the Oregon Historical Society Library, the Oregon Collection in the University of Oregon Library, the Tillamook County Historical Society, the Archives at Oregon State University, the Multnomah County Library, the Folklore Archives in the English Department at the University of Oregon, the Umatilla County Library, the La Grande City Library, the Union City Library, the Union County Historical Society, the Southern Oregon Historical Society, the Douglas County Museum, the Lincoln County Historical Society, the Oregon Shakespearean Theatre, the Columbia River Maritime Museum, and the Oregon State Library.

Finally, to my family, thank you. Thank you for travelling with me all those extra miles to view just one more haunted house or just one more spooky place; thank you Malindi, Polly and Luke, for that delightful day in the summer when we scrambled together through the brambles, searching for the Conser Lake Monster; thank you all for listening as I read you the stories and thank you for asking to hear some of them again; and thank you Christine, for everything.

For Gladys Hamley Horne,
Who showed me the books
and
told me to write.

Table of Contents

Foreword..1
Rue, Ghostly Lady of Heceta Head.....................3
Haunted Homestead on the Siuslaw River...........17
The Haunted Lighthouse at Newport...................19
Ghost Ship at Bayocean....................................35
Waldport's Haunted House................................38
A Ghost Guards the Treasure on Neahkahnie
    Mountain..39
The Monster in Devil's Lake............................43
The Klamath Lady...44
The Singing Ghost...44
The Ghost of Tillamook Light...........................45
The Ghost in Lithia Park.................................53
The Troll of Horny Chessman...........................54
The Ghost of Charles Laughton........................54
Bandage Man...55
The Ghost in Battery Russell...........................67
Ghost Ship on the Columbia Bar......................68
The Phantom Bugler..70
The Ghost of the John Day Fording..................71
Lemures in Mount Ashland..............................72
The Ghost in the Umatilla County Library.........73
Lavender...74
Hot Lake Hotel...79
The Monster in Wallowa Lake..........................89
The Laughing Devil in Laughing Devil Canyon.....98
The Steens Mountain Ghost..............................99

The Ghost of Enchanted Prairie.........................102
The Haunted McAlder Homestead........................113
The Galesville Hotel..................................114
The Hunchback of Lithia Park..........................120
Haunted Houses of Jacksonville........................121
The Ghost of Grizzly Gulch............................129
Applegate House.......................................129
The Ghost of George Harding...........................136
The Ghost in South Eugene High School
　　　Auditorium.......................................136
The Conser Lake Monster...............................142
Index...154

Foreword

In Wallowa County they talk about a monster "as long as a rowboat" with "a head like a hog's head", and "eyes about 14 inches apart", that lives in Wallowa Lake. Near La Grande, in an old hotel, a piano plays and a woman screams in the night--but, except for the listener, the hotel is empty. In the attic of a lovely old house on Heceta Head, just above the pounding Pacific, Rue, an old lady in an old-fashioned dress, floats, legless, toward a terrified workman. Near Albany, a tall, shaggy creature rises from a swamp and lopes down the road beside a mint truck, peering curiously through the driver's window, and staying alongside the truck at speeds up to 35 miles per hour.

There are ghosts and monsters in Oregon, and this is a collection of stories about them.

I gathered some of the stories naturally, as a penny-winkle gathers little rocks and pine needles, by living in Oregon. A lot of stories come your way in forty-one years. Others, I sought out, especially for this book, an effort which began in the fall of 1979. Since that time I have traveled round the state several times, asking, mainly in libraries but sometimes in taverns and grocery stores, for ghost stories or monster stories--the local legends with which this book is filled.

Some of the stories I picked up from other publications and republished. Others I retold. Still others are interviews I conducted with people who have had some strange experiences. And some came to me as unconnected fragments, which I wove together to

1

form new, complete stories.

Are these, then, true stories? Some are, without doubt. All of the people I interviewed were truthful, honest people, and I am convinced that they spoke only the truth when they spoke with me. Every story in this book has, at the very least, a strain of truth running through it, a basis in someone's personal experience. I did not track each of the stories to its original source, though, and, as is the way with stories of ghosts and monsters, embellishment may have occurred in the retelling or reconstruction of those that came to me third or fourth hand or as a series of unconnected fragments.

The point of the book, though, is that there are ghosts and monsters in Oregon. The sum of the evidence is too great to deny.

When you've read this book, you will not only believe in the existence of Oregon's ghosts and monsters, you'll know where to find them.

Mike Helm
Eugene, Oregon
October 31, 1983

Rue,
Ghostly Lady
of
Heceta Head

A light tower and a lonely old white house
stand above the Pacific on a lovely rugged headland
a few miles north of Florence, Oregon. Bruno Heceta,
a captain in the Royal Navy of Spain, first recorded
the existence of this headland in the spring of 1775.
Heceta was on a secret voyage of exploration, bound
for the 65th parallel, under orders to "...land often,
take possession, erect a cross and plant a bottle con-
taining a record of the act of possession." His scur-
vy-plagued voyage fell short of its mark, but he did
discover the mouth of the Columbia River, and made
note of this headland and the shallow water extend-

3

ing offshore, both of which now bear his name.

In 1889, because of the increasing flow of commerce along the Oregon coast, the U. S. Senate passed a bill providing $80,000 for the construction of a light station at Heceta Head. The plans for the station were duplicates of the ones used for the Umpqua light station, and included the light tower, two oil houses, a barn, a single dwelling for the head keeper, and a duplex for two assistants. Contracts for construction of the buildings were awarded in 1892 and, on March 30, 1894, the first match was applied to the coal oil lamp. The light generated 80,000 candle power and was visible for 20 miles. This was the last major light station constructed on the Oregon coast, and it houses Oregon's most powerful beacon.

Today's traveller best glimpses Heceta Head from the south, from a wide place in the Pacific Coast Highway, just north of Sea Lion Caves. Heceta House and the lighthouse tower arrest the vision, both standing dramatically above the deep blue or gray of the Pacific. From dusk to dawn the light in the tower revolves, but, during daylight hours, it is the house that holds the traveler's attention.

It glistens, this old house. Perched above the sea in shiny white contrast to the surrounding brush and rock, the caretaker's house on Heceta Head has shown its face to the Pacific Ocean for more than ninety years. It is an elegant old house, built in a time when great attention was paid to artistic architectural detail. Once it was a duplex, built to house the first and second assistant lighthouse keepers and their families. The head lighthouse keeper lived in a similar, single, house next door, a few steps nearer the lighthouse.

The keepers and the elegant single house are gone. The lighthouse remains, but the light is electric now, and it runs automatically, monitored by radio from the Coast Guard Station in Florence. The single house was torn down in 1940, the lumber used to build a store in Mapleton, now called the Alpha-bit

4

Cafe. The barn, too, is gone, and now the only major building remaining on the headland is Heceta House, the stately, splendid, isolated former duplex.

Heceta House is haunted. Owned by the Forest Service and leased to Lane Community College, its human occupants since 1973 have been Harry and Ann Tammen, who are employed by the college as caretakers, and dozens, or perhaps hundreds, of LCC students and teachers who use the old house as a coastal classroom and retreat. The Tammens, their guests, students, workmen, and others who have spent time in the old house, encounter from time to time a withered old lady who floats across rooms, screams in the night, rattles dishes in cupboards, passes through closed doors, moves tools from one place to another and makes strange noises in the night.

The withered old lady of Heceta House is known as Rue, a name spelled out in the house on a Ouija board one night. An old picture shows the house with a tombstone on the front lawn, and some speculate that Rue was the wife of an early-day lighthouse keeper, the unhappy mother of a baby who died and was buried in front of the house in the early days. Some workmen who have encountered Rue feel that her chief concern is with the house, that she stays around to make sure that they take good care of "her" house.

Harry and Ann Tammen have lived in Heceta House since 1973. They are sensible, no-nonsense people who don't believe in ghosts. Yet, there are some things... Well, listen in here to an interview that took place in October, 1979:

(The interview took place in the Tammens' kitchen, a large well-lit room on the ground floor of Heceta House. Harry and Ann and I sat around the kitchen table drinking coffee and talking. My tape recorder captured the conversation.)

5

Harry: ...let me preface this by saying that we don't, per se, believe in ghosts--but there were strange things, we always heard weird things and there were feelings and sensations in this house that we didn't equate to ghosts. It's just a weird old house. We're Los Angeles people. Lived there seventeen years and suddenly came up here and were dumped in a lighthouse. By fate. And, uh, we didn't ever put it together with any psychic phenomena or anything like that.

Then Jim Alexander, who was hired by the Forest Service, to do several repairs in the house, which amounted to about $14,000, got so terrified by what he saw in the attic, that he quit the job. It was a government contract. There's nothing easier than working on those and yet he'd walk out and said he'd never come back in this house again. Anyway, we see him down on Bay Street, he just shakes his head and says, "You're still living there, huh?" He just can't believe it.

...he had a couple of minor encounters and unexplained things like tools disappearing and stuff, but the climax came when he was up in the attic repairing a window. The attics are such that there's just a trap door. There's two attics. The house was a duplex. The attic on the other side, where he saw the...thing, had just a trap door with a ladder and to even get from the top of the ladder to the trap door...the ladder's not long enough. (The ceilings in this old house are 14 feet from the floors.) You gotta kind of chin yourself up to it, about a four foot jump up. Well, he was so terrified he forgot about the ladder. He just jumped down. (laughter) You can see how high the ceilings are in this old house.

Ann: We were sitting here and we heard this CLUMP!

Harry: By the time I got up from here after hearing the sound, he'd come down the other flight of stairs to this floor, was out the front door and in his truck with his son and his other helper, a couple

6

of kids in their twenties, and he was burning rubber out of here. We never did get an explanation till a day or two later when he came back to get his tools and stuff.

He said he was up there repairing the window, and...

Ann: He saw a reflection...

Harry: In the window, you know. Just like you look over there you see sort of a reflection. In the window--there's another one opposite him--he saw a person there and he figured his son or his helper...

"The first thing I noticed was, she's coming toward me but she's not taking steps. She's floating."

Ann: ...Leonard...

Harry: Leonard...had come up to get something or ask him something, and so he turned around, and instead of that he said it was an old woman, very, very old, wrinkle-faced woman, dressed in what he described as sort of pioneer-type clothes, very, very old-fashioned clothes, not ghostly but old fashioned

7

clothes and he said, "The first thing I noticed was, she's coming towards me but she's not taking steps. She's floating." And, mind you, this happened in possibly four, five, six seconds. The whole experience. In later recounting, it takes longer to tell. She wasn't stepping. She was floating. The dress ended about that far above the ground (holds hand about six inches off the floor) and there was no feet.

He says, "I took a step back against the wall. The trap door's right there (points to middle of kitchen) and I have to go past her to get down, and so in trying to decide what to do..."--she's still comin', comin', comin', comin' and, as she got closer, close enough to where he was just almost ready to touch her--He was really terrified, he says, by now--she started turning transparent. Just as she went, as she went, invisible, she went right on through him...

Ann: He took off...

Harry: That's when he dove out that trap door.

Ann: He went home and drew her.

Harry: He said he went home right away that day and sketched her. He does a little sketching and stuff. And that disappeared. He put it somewhere and he said to this day he can't draw it again. Just something blocking it. He had a real good drawing of her, exactly the way she looked, and he doesn't know where that went.

...that was the climax experience. These little things that led up to it were weird. He was installing doors upstairs on the other side and--I'll take you round there and show you--there's bunk beds. These college kids come out here and bring their own sleeping stuff and sleep on these GI type bunk beds. But he'd finished installing a door and he'd put his tools up here--he's working on a high level as he's working on the door and the tools are right handy, on the top bunk. He got down to install a little metal plate that goes over a lock. He had the screws in his mouth and he gets down to about this level (door-knob level) realized he needed his hammer, so he got his hammer, hammered it in, threw that up and reached for the

8

screwdriver he'd just put up there. That quick, it was gone. In that split second when he tossed the hammer up, every tool that he'd had on the bed was gone. And a clipboard he had. He kept a log of government...how much time to do this, how much time to do that. He had a log for the jobs he was doing. Gone. In the flick of an eye.

Mike: Wow. Did he find them?

Harry: Well, his son and his helper, 20, 22 year old kids, were outside painting. And this was before the ghost thing. He assumed they'd played a trick on him, So he went out, "All right. Come on. Leonard. Dave. Either of you been in here screwing around?"

"No."

"All right. Come on now." He told them to explain how the tools had gone. "You're crazy," they told him.

So they both came with him, they go in the room and they look around. His son goes in the next bedroom, around the corner in the next bedroom, he says "You idiot. They're in here on this bed." And there they were, laid out almost exactly the same way he remembered them being laid out, but on a different bed in a different room. But the clipboard didn't come back. As if they went somewhere and when she or he or it or whatever it was that was through with them, they were put back but in the wrong room. They kept the clipboard. Never did find it.

...He was working in the garage on some storm windows. He took them in there because it started to rain. And he had some other tools literally, that quick, disappear before his eyes, practically. Lay something down. Gone.

Ann: She didn't like him. (laughs)

Harry: Well, yeah. So then he came back and told us about that experience, and, at that point wasn't psyched out enough not to work on the house, but said he wouldn't go back inside the house. So they had scaffolding up outside, and he started painting again. In looking in the front of the window that

9

he'd been repairing, there she is again. Looking right out at him. He looked good and hard, long. It's the same woman and he felt a sense of security, being on the outside, and he said, something just told him, quit. He got out, and that's when he left. Two or three days after seeing her up in the attic. When he saw her the second time, looking through the window, he just walked off the job. Said, that's it. He's a contractor, well known in Florence.

Ann: Well they had knocked out two back windows, too. And he'd left the glass upstairs.

Harry: The thing he was fixing when he saw her was some windows that had gotten broken from the outside in. They swung a ladder at them. The broken glass was still all over the attic.

Now, we rarely go up to the attic. Just rats and everything else up there. The place is dirty. We didn't have any reason to use that part of the house. They're huge attics.

Well, about a week after he quit the job--and he'd told us what happened--I didn't equate it with the glass or anything, exactly ten minutes after two one night, we both wake up, just, suddenly hear a strange sound, right?

Right smack over our bedroom, where we sleep, is right where the glass was. The back windows look out there, they'd got hit in and there was glass scattered over an eight or ten foot area, which was right smack over where our bed is, the bedroom that we sleep in, on the second floor. And we heard this strange sound. Just weird. We'd heard other sounds, but this one was weirder. (whispers) sweep. sweep. sweep.

It was a broom on the old wood floor of the attic, and you'd hear the little tinkle of the glass. Just scritch, scritch, scrrritch. Sweeping. Ten minutes, we're both talking. Don't like going up there in the dark (laughter). We sat there and laid awake. It stopped in about ten minutes, and the reason I looked at the clock is when you wake up suddenly like that you think, did the alarm go off? No. It was ten after

10

"So they had some scaffolding up outside, and he started painting again. In looking in...the (attic) window he'd been repairing, there she is again. Looking right out at him..." (Rainy Day Press Photo)

two when it started and it lasted for about ten minutes, the sweeping.

Ann: That's the definite time of the night,
though.

Harry: Definitely sweeping. A broom. That's
exactly the sound it makes. We picked up the glass a
year and a half later (and we listened to each other
sweep). She went downstairs and I swept, I went
downstairs and she swept.

But the next morning, soon as the alarm went
off, I shot up the stairs. Now it's light I'm brave.
Shot up the stairs. All this broken glass, and I checked with him (the contractor) and he had not cleaned
it up, it was neatly swept into a pile about that big
around.

Ann: No brush around.

Harry: There was no broom up there. The attic's locked. Nobody in the house but us. And here it
was a perfect--and it was so dusty up there that it
was as if she'd used a real old fashioned broom because the glass was swept up so the broom marks
were in the filth up there. You know, like you'd
swept really heavy with an old fashioned hearth
broom or something.

Well, at that point we weren't (yet)... be-
lievers...

Ann: Getting close...

Harry: I just didn't have the heart to touch
that up there. As the years went by nothing else as
dramatic happened. Just a lot of little tiny things but
nothing dramatic. I got the courage and we needed
the space and I cleaned it up. No dire consequences.
We just sort of expanded into the attic to put some
of our junk up there.

Ann: Well, the other thing we heard at two
o'clock in the morning was ping pong balls. Weird.
That ping pong ball noise, knowing now that we have
packrats in that attic up there, I'd almost rather set
that down as one of their tricks...

Harry: From where, though?

Ann: I don't know, because there was no ping

12

pong ball when we went up there. But we do have packrats and you can hear them coming...

Harry: We went up and checked. This was another wakeup thing. And this was about two thirty, roughly two thirty. All of the things that happened seemed to happen between two to three. Including the house getting hot.

Ann: It's unbearably hot up in our bedroom.

Mike: Does that still happen?

Harry: Yeah.

Ann: Stifling.

Harry: Right now you probably think the heat's not on and it's coolish. What's the temperature in here?

Ann: Sixty-six.

Harry: Ann and I don't like too much heat, so we keep the heat down. Unless there are classes here. We have classes here every weekend.

Ann: College kids.

Harry: Yeah. The house gets hot when they're here, but during the week we just keep it off unless it's really a cold night and it can be 66, 65 degrees. We'll go to bed and wake up in the middle of the night and it'll be 85. Hot. Uncomfortably hot. Usually it's the opposite. They say haunted houses are cold. This place has the reverse of that phenomena. Two or three times a month. I've checked the thermometer. 85, 86 degrees, when it's blowing and windy outside.

This ping pong ball she's talking about woke us up. It was as if someone had taken a ping pong ball as high as these ceilings are--and the attic's even higher--and that first pop is what did it. POP. Woke up. Pop----pop---pop--pop-poppopopopopop. I mean like it was really dropped from a height and that first bounce...

Ann: Well you know how one sounds when it falls off a table...

Mike: Sure.

Harry: There's no ping pong table or balls in this house. We tried right on the spot to find out

13

what it was. We went right up in the attic and we looked everywhere. No sign of it. Nothing. But it was right over our bed again.

    Mike: Have you ever seen anything?

    Harry: Yes. And the students have seen things.

(One night two girls were sitting around the house and they both saw something that looked to them like a puff of smoke moving up the staircase. Another student saw an old woman in an old fashioned coat suddenly materialize on the porch. The old woman was looking into the house through a window in the living room where the student was sitting with a group.)

    Harry: I saw it, or her, or part of her one night.

We had friends in from Yachats and I had (to get) something from my car and my car keys were up in my bedroom. And just before they left we were sitting around talking...I went dashing up the stairs...As I rounded the last bend up there...like I caught her off guard, like she was hanging over the railings, literally. I saw a skirt. Right there in front of me. And I jumped so fast...and in that split second that skirt from dead still went phwisssshhhht and went through a door that was locked that goes into one of the bedrooms that then goes into the attic. And I grabbed the key. My keys are inside on the same ring as the car keys. Looked around in our bedroom. I didn't know what it was. Opened that door, looked around in there. Nothing. Nothing around. She went right through that door. All I saw was a skirt. Dark gray skirt. Just a skirt. Whhhishhht. Gone.

    Ann: What I saw was clearer than that. I saw a full person. Right here. We had people here to dinner. And I was clearing the table. I was carrying the dishes from in there (the dining room) to in here (the kitchen)...As I started back about the second time, I'm going out through this way as I see somebody coming through this (the other) way, and I thought,

"Darnit. I told them to sit down." And I got into the other room and both the gals are still sitting there. But I saw something in this door, with something in her hand. And I was getting mad at my guests because I thought they were getting up to help me and it was somebody else, obviously, because I came back around the corner to see who it was. And there was nobody there. But I'm sure I saw something...

And I wasn't drinking a thing that night. I was the most sober one in the crowd, because the doctor told me I couldn't drink.

Harry: Nobody was drinking anything anyway.

Ann: But to see something standing there or moving towards the kitchen and it looks like she's carrying something. A definite woman's shape...

Harry and Ann Tammen still don't believe in ghosts, but they have evolved at theory which may help to explain the unexplainable in another way.

Harry: I feel there is another dimension that we don't know about...time being a dimension...(and)... We wonder if there isn't a little short circuit in time, and what we're seeing, or the ghost that Jim Alexander saw, wasn't October 27, 1899, for a split second. And perhaps...

Mike: Simultaneously, but at different times. That sounds like a contradiction, but it isn't.

Harry: No. Because the dimensions are there. All stacked up. We're here. We exist. Our energy or whatever you want to call it, our vibrations, are here. And...this has to go on...

Heceta House is now protected by its designation as a National Historic Site. When I spoke again with Harry Tammen in the fall of 1983, he told me that nearly $250,000 in grants had been designated to finance a ten-year restoration project for the gracious old house. By 1993, portions of the house that

15

were torn down during World War II will have been rebuilt and the house completely restored to its former grandeur.

The Ghost in the Trees
near Tutuilla Mission

Some say that the ghost of an Indian lady hovers in the trees outside this house near Tutuilla Mission east of Pendleton, and that she can occasionally be seen, late at night, peering into the upstairs front window. (Rainy Day Press Photo)

The Haunted Homestead
on the
Siuslaw River

There's some land down on the Siuslaw River that's so spooky the cows won't even graze on it.

In the early part of this century a family with five children lived on the south bank of the Siuslaw River near Florence. They owned a farm of 40 or 50 acres and their home was a snug little cabin in a canyon on the river bank. One terrible winter during the 1920s the rain-sodden walls of the canyon caved in. A vast wall of mud slid down over the little cabin and into the Siuslaw. Six of the seven members of the family were killed in the mudslide and the course of the Siuslaw was changed by the mass of earth suddenly dumped into its middle.

Today the wind howls eerily through the canyon and, some say, anguished voices can be heard beneath the ground where the little cabin once stood.

The Yaquina Bay Lifesaving Service was housed
in the old lighthouse from 1906 until 1933. Sometime
during those years this photo was taken. Three
people dressed for a Sunday outing are seated, but
barely visible, on Whale Rock, in the foreground.
(Photo courtesy of Oregon Historical Society)

The Haunted Lighthouse at Newport

The following story is based on "The Haunted Light at Newport by the Sea", written by Lischen M. Miller and originally published in **Pacific Monthly,** Volume II, 1899. Miller's story was reprinted by The Lincoln County Historical Society in July, 1973.

ZINA TREVENARD
AND THE GHOST OF EVAN MACCLURE

Part 1: The Old Deserted Lighthouse

The old lighthouse in Newport marks the location of the first land charted by white men in the Pacific Northwest. The landfall was made by Captain James Cook, aboard the "Resolution" on March 7, 1778. Cook was on a voyage around the world, the primary purpose of which was to discover the Straits of Anian, the legendary short-cut by water through North America from Europe to the Orient. Because of the heavy spring weather, Cook was unable to approach close enough to find a harbor on the Oregon coast. He remained off the Oregon coast for six days, during which time he named and charted Cape Gregory, Cape Perpetua, and Cape Foulweather.

Cook's visit stimulated the interest of the colonial powers in the Pacific Northwest. John Ledyard, an American who accompanied Cook, later visited Thomas Jefferson in Paris and was instrumental in arousing Jefferson's interest in the area. This led to the Louisiana Purchase in 1803 and the dispatch in the same year of the Lewis and Clark expedition, the first American exploration west of the Rocky Mountains.

The lighthouse was the first major aid to navigation constructed in the area of Cook's landfall. It was built during the summer of 1871 and lighted on November 3 of that year. It is the second oldest lighthouse in Oregon, and the oldest building of its kind still standing on the Oregon coast. It was used as a navigational aid for just under three years. When the lighthouse on Yaquina Head, just three miles north of Yaquina Bay, began operation in 1874, the whale oil lamp in the lighthouse at Yaquina Bay was extinguished forever.

During the past 100 years the old lighthouse has been used at times to house Coast Guardsmen, Army engineers, and caretakers for Yaquina Bay State Park, but, during most of that time it has been uninhabited, at least by humans.

Part 2: 1873--Oregon's
Wandering Coastal Ghost

Evan MacClure, violent captain of the American whaler Moncton, loved nothing more ashore than a good brawl--especially when there was a prize involved, and most especially when the prize was a pretty girl. MacClure made a big mistake, though, when his eyes and his fancy fell on Lehui Opakahini, who was known through out the whaling fleet as the Queen of the Whalers' Arms.

Lehui, legend has it, was already betrothed, at least while he was in port, to big Bill Brewster, the fat, jocular first mate of the Moncton. This informal arrangement meant nothing to MacClure, whose habit it was to let nothing stand between himself and the object of his desire.

The confrontation came in the Whalers' Arms on the second afternoon of the Moncton's stopover in Honolulu in 1873. Brewster, a fleshy giant with dry flaxen hair and mottled, unhealthy-looking skin, sat drinking with a few members of the Moncton's crew. His big pale hand was wrapped around a mug of Wha-

20

lers' Ale, and one flabby arm was draped carelessly around Lehui's shoulders when Evan MacClure strode through the swinging doors of the tropical saloon.

Brewster, in an expansive mood, shouted a welcome to his captain, and invited MacClure to join the group at his table for a mug of ale. MacClure's cold eyes swept around the Whalers' Arms and stopped when they fell upon the lovely Lehui. He walked straight to Brewster's table and sat down, all the time looking directly at Lehui. MacClure didn't seem to see Brewster, but Brewster saw, in an uncomfortable hurry, that he had a problem.

"Now, just hold on there, Captain," he said, sensing the inevitable and drawing his arm tighter around Lehui's shoulders.

"Brewster," MacClure said, still not looking at the first mate, "I mean to have this woman." The wild-eyed, muscle-bound MacClure could inspire fear in a full-grown grizzly bear. The level, cold tone of his voice that afternoon was calculated to inspire just that emotion in the first mate. It worked.

"Now, C'mon, Captain," Brewster whined. "Hula's my girl. Ain't ya, Hula."

Lehui's nickname was inspired by the manner in which she performed the traditional dance of the islands. When Hula-hui danced, missionaries and whalers alike foamed at the mouth, though, of course, for different reasons. Hula's answer to Brewster's entreaty was a noncommittal shrug. A girl in her line of work doesn't like to offend anyone.

"That settles it, then," said MacClure with a grin as he reached across the table for the hand of the lovely Lehui. "C'mon, Hula."

The great knife Brewster wore at his belt flashed in an arc. Before he could pull away, MacClure's hand was nailed to the table. The crowd moved away as the two men faced each other.

"I mean to have this woman, Brewster," MacClure reminded him, levelling his icy gaze at the first mate and ignoring the knife that held his hand, palm down, fast to the table.

"She's mine, Captain," Brewster responded, readying himself for the attack he knew was coming.

"Very well." MacClure's dead level tone was the quiet hiss of a fuse.

It was all over in an instant. MacClure jerked his hand free, threw the table aside, and went after the first mate like a buzz saw. When the furniture and bodies and bottles stopped flying, Brewster lay unconscious, a puddle of blood and beer spreading slowly around him on the rough plank floor. MacClure stood over him, thoughtfully chewing something and wrapping a large red kerchief around his bleeding hand. Finally, he spat a bloody glob on to the chest of the man at his feet.

"C'mon, Hula," he said, quietly, extending his hand in her direction. She followed him to the door. He stopped. A smile creased his face. "Wait."

He walked back to where Brewster lay on the floor and retrieved the grisly blob from the unconscious man's chest. Then, using Brewster's knife, he pinned it to the wall of the saloon. "Let's go," he said.

It was nearly an hour before Brewster became fully conscious, and quite some time after that before he realized that the bloody thing his knife held to the saloon wall was his own left ear.

Brewster never got mad, but he always got even. He sailed from Honolulu with the Moncton, assuming his position as first mate. For nearly five weeks he and MacClure worked together as though nothing had happened between them. During their fifth week at sea, though, it became brutally apparent to MacClure that Brewster had neither forgotten nor forgiven.

The first gray light of dawn was streaking the eastern sky when MacClure heard a light knock on his cabin door.

"C'min," he grumbled, pulling himself from a deep sleep.

The door burst open and a dozen or so crewmen, brandishing pistols, knives, and blubber hooks, followed the smiling Brewster into the captain's tiny compartment.

"Mornin', Captain," Brewster said politely as the crewmen crowded around the captain's bunk.

"Can we kill 'im now?" asked a sailor, jabbing the astonished captain with his pistol.

"No." Brewster said it quietly and firmly. The seaman drew back and the captain saw that Brewster was firmly in command. "We thought you might like to take a little boat ride this morning, Captain," Brewster grinned. "Lovely mornin'," he added.

Evan MacClure was never seen alive again, but a small boat like the one in which he was set adrift pitched up on the rocks near Devil's Punchbowl during a violent storm in January, 1874.

The mutineers dragged the captain from his bed to the deck of the whaling vessel, where he was put into a small boat, given some clothing, a scant amount of provisions, and a small cask of drinking water. They then lowered him to the water, cast him adrift, and sailed away, hooting derisive good-bye's as MacClure faded into the watery distance.

Evan MacClure was never seen alive again, but a small boat like the one in which he was set adrift pitched up on the rocks near Devil's Punchbowl during a violent storm in January of 1874. Accounts of the event say that a group of people watching the storm from a nearby cliff saw a man with red hair and a "face like a skeleton" climb out of the boat and stand on the rocks for a moment. A huge wave then broke over the boat and the man, washing them back into the ocean. The boat was later retrieved, but the body was never found.

A strange spring followed the appearance of the little boat and its vanishing passenger in 1874. Odd lights were seen and strange noises heard on the beaches. Several times lifesaving crews were called to beaches at night to answer calls for help, but no shipwrecks were sighted and no one was ever found in need of rescue. Lonely coastal dwellings suddenly became very spooky places. Chains rattled in empty cellars, windows opened and closed by themselves, chairs rocked when no one was near. Footsteps trudged across empty attics, groans and calls for help came from empty front porches. Some houses became so cold that no amount of firewood could warm them. Others, even on cold nights, were so warm that the windows and doors were thrown open to cool them.

From this abundance of ghostly occurrences grew the legend of Oregon's wandering coastal ghost. He visited lighthouses and homes, and, occasionally, turned up on sailing ships just off the coast. Once he turned up in a tavern in Newport where he ordered a beer and then vanished when it was served. The bartender fainted.

24

On October 1, 1874, the light was extinguished, the lighthouse deserted. Oregon's wandering coastal ghost, that of Evan MacClure, legend has it, moved right in and he's been there ever since. (Photo Courtesy of Oregon Historical Society)

As the year grew on, the ghost began to materialize more and more often. He was always described as a red-haired man in sailor's dress, with a
skull-like face. He once confided to a terrified farmer's wife that he needed two things before he could
rest: a place to stay and someone to join him in his
ghostly exile.

On October 1, 1874, the U. S. Lighthouse Service officially closed down the Yaquina Bay Lighthouse. The light was extinguished, the lighthouse
keeper packed his bags, and the building, just three
years old but already showing the effects of exposure
to the heavy coastal weather, was deserted.

The ghost of Evan MacClure, legend has it,
was delighted. He moved right in and he's been there
ever since.

Part 3: 1874--Zina Trevenard

The first winter storms in early November of
1874 brought a strange sloop over the bar into Yaquina Bay. Described by a historian of the time as
"grotesquely rigged", the sloop was commanded by a
"beetle-browed ruffian with a scar across his cheek
from mouth to ear" and manned by a "swarthy crew"
who spoke a "heathenish, unfamiliar language". The
sloop dropped anchor in the bay and a boat was lowered and rowed toward the strip of sandy beach
where almost the entire population of Newport village had gathered to witness this uncommon event.

In the boat was a man of about 40 and his beautiful young daughter. The man had the manners of a
gentleman and was treated with great respect by the
crewmen in the boat. He explained that the sloop's
water casks were empty and that he would like to
fill them before the sloop continued its journey.
When he received directions to a spring in a cliff a
few hundred yards up the beach, he relayed the information to the crew, speaking to them in the unfamiliar tongue. The crew then went off for water,
leaving the man and his daughter with the townspeo-
ple.

26

The man, whose name, he said, was Trevenard, cast a critical eye toward the collection of rude wooden huts and the small Indian camp that made up Newport at that time, and spent the next half hour or so asking questions. Then, satisfied with the character of the place, the man had a proposal for the villagers. The sloop, he said, was bound for Coos Bay and would be passing up the coast again in a couple of weeks. The rough seas had upset Zina, his lovely daughter, as she was not a good sailor. Therefore, if a suitable place could be found for her to stay in Newport, he wished to leave her until he returned.

There was a place for his daughter, the villagers assured him--the Yaquina Bay Hotel. After conferring with the landlady of the hotel, the man ordered Zina's luggage brought ashore and kissed her good-bye. He was rowed quickly back to the mysterious sloop, which immediately weighed anchor and sailed into the sunset.

Though Zina had the appearance, manners, and possessions of a princess, she adjusted gracefully to the inconveniences of frontier life, and was soon accepted by the people of Newport as one of their own. She was a girl with an artistic inclination, and, on days when the weather was fair, she spent many hours sketching seaside scenes, writing poetry, and walking along the beaches near Newport.

Two weeks stretched into four and then into six, and still the strange sloop did not return. "Don't worry," the landlady told her. "Your father's safe enough. No rough weather since he sailed, and as for time--a ship's time is as uncertain as a woman's temper, I've heard my own father say."[1]

"I am not worried," Zina replied. "Not at all." Indeed, it was as if she did not expect her father to return.

Christmas week in 1874 brought fair weather to the Oregon coast. No place in Oregon is as pleasant as the coast on those rare winter days when the wind holds its icy breath and the sun glistens low in a cloudless sky. A group of young people came from

27

the Willamette Valley for a coastal respite from the inland winter rains. They took up rooms in the Yaquina Bay Hotel and almost immediately became friendly with Zina Trevenard.

The group frolicked on the beach, explored the tide pools and coastal caves, fished in the surf and hiked the grassy areas upland from the beach. Great bonfires were built from driftwood on the beach each evening and the young people gathered in the fire's warm glow to sing songs and tell stories.

One afternoon the suggestion was made that they explore the abandoned lighthouse that stands like a lonely sentinel at the mouth of Yaquina Bay.

"It's just an ordinary house," Zina told them, "with a light tower built on the back. It's probably locked up, but if we could get in, we could get a good view from there."

The key was in the possession of the hotel landlady, who gave it to the young people and warned them against staying around the lighthouse after dark. Almost everyone in Newport had heard tales of nocturnal noises and weird lights emanating from the lighthouse since the lighthouse keeper moved out. The landlady had heard the stories and, though she said she did not believe in ghosts, she had an ominous feeling as she watched the young people set off toward the lighthouse.

The day was cold and clear. Tiny, glistening wavetops spangled the bay, dazzling the eyes of the young people as the little group started off in the afternoon sunshine to climb the narrow path through the woods behind the lighthouse.

Lischen M. Miller described the scene when the group arrived at the lighthouse:

It stood in a small enclosure bare of vegetation. The sand was piled in lit-tle wind-swept heaps against the board fence. There was a walk paved with brick, leading from the gate around to the front where two or three steps went up to a square porch with seats on either side. Harold Welch unlocked the door and they went into the empty hall that echoed dismally to the sound of human voices. Rooms opened from this hallway on either hand and in the L at the back of the kitchen, storerooms and a pantry, a door that gave egress to a narrow veranda, and another shutting off the cellar. At the rear of the hall the stairs led up to the second floor which was divided like the first into plain square rooms. But the stairway went on, winding up to a small landing where a window looked out to northward, and from which a little room, evidently a linen closet, opened opposite the window. There was nothing extraordinary about this closet at the first glance. It was well furnished with shelves and drawers, and its only unoccupied wall space $_2$was finished with a simple wainscoting.^{2}

One of the boys noticed that the wainscoting appeared to be loose. He gave it a little tug and it came off in his hand. "The house," he said, "is falling to pieces."

Behind the wainscoting lay an iron panel. "It's hollow," said Zina, tapping it. "I wonder what's behind it."

Harold Welch stepped up and in an instant removed the panel, a piece of iron about three feet square. He lay the iron square aside and peered into the tunnel disclosed by its removal. "Weird," he said. "I wonder where it goes."

The tunnel led back about six or eight feet and then dropped abruptly straight down. Harold Welch crawled into the tunnel, carrying some crumpled pieces of paper. He set them on fire and dropped them into the shaft. "It goes clear down to the ocean," he said, backing out and brushing the cobwebs and dirt from his clothes.

"Wonder what it's for," said Zina, peering into the dark passage.

"Maybe the ghost stashes bodies in there," suggested one of the boys.

"Maybe smugglers use it," suggested another.

The members of the little group laughed, nervously now, for their mood had undergone a change as they crowded together in the linen closet. The gaiety of the early afternoon was suddenly replaced with an odd, heavy foreboding. Gone also was the brilliant sunshine, for, as they explored the deserted lighthouse, a thick fog had crept in from the sea, enveloping the old place in a heavy gray shroud.

"Let's get out of here," whispered one of the girls. They all agreed. Without a word, they clambered as one down the steps and out the back door.

Harold Welch had the key and the rusty old lock proved difficult to manipulate this time. By the time he had coerced it into performing, the rest of the group was far down the path in the trees. When he turned from the door he was surprised to see Zina waiting for him.

"Thank you for waiting."

She smiled and put her hand on his arm. "I left my handkerchief in there, and I must go back in and get it."

Harold wrestled again with the balky old lock. The door creaked open. He stood aside to let her pass into the lighthouse, and then started to follow her.

"Stop," she said, putting her hand on his. "I am going alone. Don't wait for me. Lock this door and I will come out through the kitchen."

He argued, but she prevailed. She turned and disappeared into the stairwell and he went to the back porch. The old lock was stubborn once again, and it took him several minutes to make it work. By the time he got to the rear of the house, Zina was nowhere to be seen. He called to her several times, but she did not answer, and he concluded that she had finished her business inside before he got the door locked and had hurried on down the hill to join the rest of the group. He ran on down the path.

"Where's Zina?" he asked when he caught up with the group.

"Don't you know?" one of them asked, surprised. "She was with you when we last saw her."

"She went back into the lighthouse to get her handkerchief. She wouldn't let me go with her, so I locked the door and came on. I thought she had come out the kitchen door ahead of me."

"She can't get out the kitchen door," said one of the boys. "I tried it. The door's locked and the key's broken off in the lock."

"Then she's locked in that horrid place," cried one of the girls.

The group had just turned toward the lighthouse when a horrible shriek ripped through the fog. As one they bolted up the path. Three more anguished screams for help came from the direction of the lighthouse, then nothing more.

"We're coming, Zina," called Welch. "Don't be afraid." There was no reply.

They reached the back porch and Harold Welch again struggled with the rusty old lock. At last, he threw the door open and they poured into the lighthouse. They searched the lower rooms and, finding nothing, ran upstairs. On the floor in one of the upper bedrooms, they found a pool of warm, red blood. Drops of blood spattered the stairs and a small handkerchief lay in the closet where they had discovered the hidden tunnel. The panel, to their horror, had been replaced, as had been the wainscoting. Try as they might, they could not pry it loose.

They ran to the village and gave the alarm. Villagers came to the lighthouse and searched once again, this time with lanterns, but to no avail. The next day they searched the surrounding beaches and hillocks, in the hope that she might have become disoriented in her terror and wandered the wrong way in the fog. They found only the blood and a little

31

handkerchief. The lovely Zina had disappeared.

The sloop which carried Zina and her father to Newport never reappeared in Yaquina Bay, and no record can be found of its visit anywhere else on the Oregon coast. Where Zina came from is a mystery.

The bloodstains, though, on the floor in the upstairs bedroom of the old deserted lighthouse, are no mystery. They are still there today.

Part 4: Just Last Summer

Just after dusk one evening early last summer, a hitch-hiker, thumbing his way north on Highway 101, said good-bye to his last ride of the day on the outskirts of Newport. Though he had no money, he carried with him enough food for an evening meal. He looked for a sheltered and secluded spot where he could roll out his sleeping bag for the night.

Walking toward the ocean, he came to the deserted Yaquina Bay lighthouse. Curious, he climbed the concrete stairs from the roadway to have a look at the old relic, but, halfway up, he found his way blocked by a high, chain-link fence. Just through the fence, near the front door to the old lighthouse, was just the sort of place he had in mind to spend the night.

He threw his backpack and bedroll over the fence and climbed into the enclosure to make his camp. From a few sticks and twigs he made a small campfire, over which he warmed a can of pork and beans. He ate his meal straight from the can on the flat of the large blade in his Swiss Army knife and washed it down with a couple of swallows from a jug of white wine. Satisfied, he rolled out his sleeping bag and lay on his back in the lee of the old lighthouse, contemplating the bright summer sky and the powerful roar of the Pacific.

The hitch-hiker was troubled by his lack of money and by the fact that he'd just eaten his last can of beans. Though he had tried, as he travelled north, for an occasional job, he had so far been unable to find anyone willing to hire him. His last thought, before sleep blotted out the night, was that, unless he experienced a radical change of luck, the next day promised only hunger and frustration.

Sometime later he was awakened by the click of the latch in the front door to the lighthouse. He sat up in his sleeping bag and saw that the windows in the old place now glowed. The interior was bathed in a soft, yellow light. The lighthouse tower, barely visible from where he sat on the ground, also appeared to be lit.

The door opened and a young woman in a white, floor-length dress appeared on the porch. A man stood in the doorway behind her. She quietly descended the stairs and walked lightly across the grass toward the hitch-hiker. The man remained on the porch.

The hitch-hiker sat up in his sleeping bag, embarrassed at being discovered asleep on what he now believed was the young lady's front lawn.

"Don't worry, Harold," she said softly, "you are welcome here."

He looked more closely at the lady he now believed to be his hostess, but he could not quite make out her features in the darkness.

"Thank you, Ma'am," he said, "but I'm not Harold. I thought this place was deserted. I had no idea that anyone still lived here or," he gestured up at the light in the tower, "that the light was still in use."

To this she did not reply. Instead, she stood over the man for a few moments. Though he could not see her eyes, he felt her peering down at him. It felt, he later remembered, like she was looking right into her thoughts.

"I see you are worried," she said at last. "Do not worry. In the morning you will find work in Newport. That job will give you sufficient money and food to complete your journey."

With this she turned, moved smoothly across the grass and up the stairs to the front porch of the lighthouse. The man, a great, shaggy figure in the odd lamplight, turned from the doorway and vanished into the lighthouse. In the doorway the young woman paused to look once again toward the hitch-hiker. He noticed that she carried with her an aura of soft light. Then she followed the man inside and the door closed softly behind them.

The hitch-hiker was suddenly very tired. He snuggled back into his sleeping bag and slept soundly until morning.

During the night the skipper of a northbound Sause Brothers tugboat radioed the U. S. Coast Guard from a point about two miles off the entrance to Yaquina Bay to say that he could see light shining from the old abandoned lighthouse at the entrance to the bay. The pilot of a Cessna 150, following the phosphorescent roll of breakers down the coast from Astoria to Coos Bay, radioed the same observation. Coast Guardsmen on duty in the lookout tower directly behind the old lighthouse, having witnessed the mysterious phenomena many times before, received the reports in a routine manner and radioed back that they, too, could see the light coming from the lighthouse.

When the hitch-hiker awoke and saw the lighthouse in the clear light of day, it was obvious to him that the place was indeed deserted. Puzzled and a little frightened by his experience of the night before, he rolled up his sleeping bag, packed up his gear, climbed over the fence and started off toward Newport in search of work and food.

By nine o'clock that morning, true to the promise of the lady in the lighthouse, he had found both a meal and a job.

[1]Miller, Lischen M. The Haunted Light at Newport by the Sea, **Pacific Monthly**, Volume II, 1899. Reprinted by Lincoln County Historical Society, Newport, Oregon, 1973.

[2]Ibid.

Ghost Ship
at Bayocean

"The coastal resort of Bayocean was a dream of man shattered by the reality of nature."
Northwest Magazine
April 6, 1975

Bayocean began in 1906 as the dream of T. B. Potter, a millionaire real estate promoter from Kansas, vacationing in the Pacific Northwest. He visited Tillamook Spit, the four-mile-long strip of land that separates Tillamook Bay from the Pacific Ocean, to fish and hunt. Inspired by its recreational and residential possibilities, he and H. L. Chapin of Portland bought the 600-acre spit, platted 4,000 lots and renamed it Bayocean Peninsula.

By 1910 2200 lots had been sold and nearly 100 buildings and homes were built. Bayocean boasted a 40-room hotel, a pavilion where dances were held and the latest movies were shown, an elaborate natatorium with a 50 x 160 foot pool, an electric plant and a gravity water system that brought clear mountain water 3 1/2 miles to the peninsula from Cape Meares. At a time when the streets of most west coast towns were still made of mud and gravel, Bayocean had miles of paved roadway.

The dream began to die in 1917, when the first noticeable erosion, about a foot a year, began to occur. Year by year the Pacific continued to chew away and, according to A Brief of the Bayocean Erosion issued by the Tillamook Chamber of Commerce, "In 1932 the erosion increased alarmingly...a choice area of ocean frontage, 100 to 200 feet in width and

35

three miles long, has been washed into the sea...roads, homes, business buildings, the natatorium were carried away and smashed to bits." The winter of 1939 saw more homes tumble into the ocean. A vicious storm that year breached the southern end of the spit, washed out huge sections of Bayocean's access road, and opened Tillamook Bay to the Pacific.

Efforts were made to repair the access road and keep the ocean from the bay, but, they were too little, too late. In 1952 an earthquake in Japan sent 50-foot waves crashing against the peninsula. The ocean gobbled more buildings, severed the water line from Cape Meares, widened the gap between the mainland and Bayocean, and crashed, unimpeded, into Tillamook Bay. The last residents of Bayocean packed what was left of their belongings and straggled across the breach at low tide to the mainland. Bayocean was dead.

In 1954 Congress authorized the Corps of Engineers to construct a 1.4 mile sand and rockfill dike along the south end of the peninsula to close the breach and prevent further erosion. The dike is there today, connecting Bayocean Peninsula, now a brushy, uninhabited sandspit, to the mainland and sheltering Tillamook Bay from the Pacific. Of the town of Bayocean, nothing remains.

I found the following article in **The Surf** Bayocean's monthly newspaper, Volume 1, Number 9, published in July, 1912:

A Phantom Ship

Whether it is the result of his new vocation of clam digging or the effect of staying up late at night in this summer city of early hours no one can say, but Geo. M. Hyland certainly had a peculiar experience last month.

It might be accounted for if the sight had been seen by him alone, but several other reputable citizens of well-known reputation were with him at the time and all stories of what happened correspond without a contradiction on any point.

Coming from Twelfth Avenue up High Terrace, a view of the ocean is not had until the hotel is reached, when the Pacific is unfolded to sight. As Mr. Hyland and several of his friends reached this spot on a night that was very dark, no stars or moon visible, they saw a peculiar and steady light on the beach

and off shore. It was too steady and brilliant to be the phosphorus, so common in this section, and while trying to find the reason of it, a full-rigged ship, in full sail, headed directly for the shore, appeared to the astonished gaze of those present. It was less than a hundred feet from the shore, sailing at full speed through a depth of water that all knew could hardly float a rowboat.

For over a minute they all gazed at this strange vessel surrounded by the unaccounted-for light, when as suddenly as it appeared, the ship was gone, as well as the lights.

Several watch parties have been looking for a repetition of this sight for several nights, but so far it has not reappeared and the "flying dutchman" is still unexplained.

The same issue of **The Surf** identifies Geo. M. Hyland as a "regular week-ender" who specialized in clam digging while the "'little' Hylands" enjoyed riding Bayocean's "burro squad...over hills and dales and beaches at all hours", and it boasts that "the changes wrought by improvements (in the last 60 days) are almost unbelievable." All the buildings were repainted white, two miles of lights were placed on Bay Street South, making "...this boulevard a favorite walk after sundown", and "hard surfacing" of roads in Bayocean now reached the ocean beach. Telephones with "...direct connection through the exchange with not only the Tillamook district, but with Portland and the Pacific Coast" were placed in additional lcoations, and the Hotel Bayocean arranged to serve bedtime lunches from ten until midnight.

Waldport's Haunted House

In a large old house over looking Waldport High School, a little black dog occasionally runs through the halls. No little black dog lives there. In the kitchen, a woman, a stranger, stands by the sink. Suddenly, she seems to "flicker in an odd light", and vanishes.

A Ghost
Guards the Treasure
on
Neahkahnie Mountain

One summer afternoon many years ago Indians near Neahkahnie Mountain were astonished to see two sailing ships approaching the coast. These were the first sailing ships ever seen along the Oregon coast and, to the Indians, they looked like "great birds" as they raced in full sail toward the shore. Suddenly, the ships drew close together, and, just beyond the breakers, they began to "thunder" and puffs of smoke issued from the gun ports in their sides. After much noise and smoke, one of the ships began to list, and was slowly but surely drawn into the breakers and cast up on the beach near the foot of the mountain. The other sailed off over the horizon and was never seen again.

As the great ship lurched onto the sand, men tumbled over its sides and staggered ashore through the surf. All of the men were white, except one, who was much larger than the others--a giant, some say. He was black. To the Indians, who assumed until then that there was only one race, these men of different colors were a frightening sight, and they regarded them much as we might regard visitors from another planet.

At low tide the strangers straggled out to their ship and began to bring their belongings ashore. A-mong the items brought from the ship was a huge chest, so heavy and cumbersome that it took eight men to carry it. With great effort, they carried the chest a short way up the the mountain, where they dug a deep hole. Carefully, they lowered the chest into the hole. The black giant, whom the Indians believed was an evil demon, was told to step forward. When he did, he was struck down, and his body was thrown into the hole on top of the chest. The men then filled the hole with sand and returned to the beach.

The Indians, as usual in their initial dealings with white people, were friendly, generous, and peaceful. They welcomed the strangers to their village, offered food, and helped the men to obtain shelter for the coming winter. The white men, as usual in their dealings with people of another race, were quick to capitalize on the generosity of their hosts. They took food, land, and other belongings from the Indians and offered venereal disease, measles, and violence in return.

The sailors quarreled with each other and with the Indians. Eventually, an Indian was killed. The Indians, retaliated, killing a white man. A balance, of sorts, was maintained in this way through two winters, but, during the third year, the tolerance of the Indians for their irascable visitors was finally exceeded.

When the sailors began, at will, to violate the Indian women, a council was held among the Clatsops, the Tillamooks, and the Nehalems. Before dawn one autumn morning, 1500 warriors crept into the camp of the white men and set fire to their dwellings. As the sailors ran from the blazing camp, the Indians killed them all. The white men were buried in a huge mound near the place where the box and the black man were buried. It is said that after this massacre, the river ran red with blood for three days.

The Indians, because of their reverence for the dead, never disturbed the burial place of the sailors, and, because of their fear of reprisal as the white presence grew in Oregon, they refrained from talking about the massacre.

Because of their fear of the "black demon", they never dug up the huge chest that the sailors buried on their beach. To this day, no one is sure what was in the chest, but many believe that the

MYSTERIOUS MARKINGS, such as these, carved into a rock found on Neahkahnie Mountain, may hold the key to the location of the legendary buried treasure. (Photo Courtesy of Tillamook County Historical Museum)

41

ship was a Spanish pirate ship and that the chest contained a fortune in gold.

Considerable evidence supports the assumption of buried treasure near Neahkahnie. In addition to the Indian legend, there are records of Spanish ships, loaded with treasure gained in raids on South American cities, sailing northward from Peru, never to be heard of again. Mysterious markings carved into the rocks on Neahkahnie Mountain could hold the key to the location of the treasure. At Three Rocks Beach, in North Lincoln County, skeletons and remnants of an old sailing vessel were found. One of the skeletons belonged to a man, thought to be a Negro, nearly eight feet tall. Stone walls, masonry and giant mounds of rocks placed in the shape of an inverted "W" with a base nearly a mile long have been discovered by treasure hunters near Neahkahnie.

If the treasure is there, it has eluded an army of treasure hunters, most of whom came to Neahkahnie with a hunch, a shovel, and a wheelbarrow. A few have come with bulldozers and backhoes. Many have come with metal detectors. Five people, including Charles and Lynn Wood, a father and son who were killed when their 30-foot deep hole caved in on them in 1931, have been killed in the search for Neahkahnie's elusive treasure.

Some say that the treasure is there, but it will never be found. They believe that the ghosts of the black giant and his evil companions still guard the treasure of Neahkahnie and that they will keep the treasure hidden, forever.

The Monster
in
Devil's Lake

The lake in northern Lincoln County that we know as Devil's Lake was known to the Indians, before the arrival of the white man, as Indian Lake.

Chief Fleetfoot, legend tells us, slipped his canoe into the water one dark night, intending to cross the lake and meet a certain young woman on the other side. Moonbeams glittered as the canoe slipped across the water. Suddenly, huge fingers, like the tentacles of a giant octopus, rose from the depths of the lake, encircled the canoe, and pulled the screaming Chief Fleetfoot beneath the surface.

The Indians, hoping to pacify the monster so they could use the lake without fear, held a feast on the lakeshore and dedicated it to the monster. Drums began to beat, and the Indians chanted, louder and louder. Suddenly a hideous head burst from the lake, a sacrifice was made, and the monster returned to the depths.

Today, Lincoln County residents will tell you, there is still a monster in Devil's Lake. In recent years it has been described as a 25-foot long catfish, a floating log covered with algae, or just algae stirred up at night by the wind. Whatever it is, the ancient Indian ceremony seems to have pacified it, because there are no recent reports of the monster claiming any victims.

The Klamath Lady

Late one night many years ago a Klamath Indian lady and her husband were crossing the Siletz River on an old swinging bridge near Siletz. The lady was carrying a baby. As they walked along the swinging bridge the man and the woman began to argue. The husband suddenly drew his knife, stabbed his wife, and threw her body and the baby off the bridge into the river. Some say the Klamath Lady turned into a white dog and haunts the road where it leads over the grade away from the river. Others believe that she is still there in her original form, a woman carrying a precious bundle, walking along the road up from the river. Pick her up, they say, and she'll ride quietly in the back of your car. She'll never let you see her face. Pass her by, and she'll make you crash.

The Singing Ghost

Some say that a tall, friendly male ghost sings madrigals ever night outside an abandoned public relations office on the third level of the Oregon Shakespearean Theatre.

The Ghost
of
Tillamook Light

"On certain nights low, chilling groans are heard
from the stair cylinder leading to the lantern..."
The History of Pacific Lighthouses
Lawrence Butcher

As maritime traffic increased along the northwest coast in the latter part of the 19th century, so
did the number of shipwrecks on and around the
mouth of the Columbia River. The toll in lives and
property caused public sentiment to grow in favor of
constructing navigational aids along the Oregon
coast, and, on June 28, 1878, Congress appropriated
$50,000 "for the purpose of constructing a first-class
lighthouse on Tillamook Head, Oregon", about 20
miles south of the entrance to the Columbia River.
The cost of building and maintaining a 20-mile road
through the wilderness to the lighthouse site on Tillamook Head, the persistence of fog and low clouds
which would obscure the view of the light from the
sea, and the danger of landslides on the headland
combined to cause the lighthouse board to look further. Major G. I. Gillespie of the U. S. Army Corps
of Engineers recommended that the lighthouse be
built on Tillamook Rock, a slippery chunk of basalt
jutting out of the Pacific a mile seaward of Tillamook Head.
The Indians knew about Tillamook Rock. They
believed it was cursed by their gods, haunted by evil

spirits, and they were never known to have approached it. The first white men to visit the rock had no cause to doubt the wisdom of the Indians' beliefs.

On June 17, 1879, H. S. Wheeler, District Superintendent of Lighthouse Construction, was ordered to Tillamook Rock and told not to return until he succeeded in landing and surveying the rock. After several tries he scrambled aboard the rock, but rough seas made it impossible for him to land his surveying instruments. With tape measure and approximation, he completed an initial survey, and the decision to build a lighthouse on this inhospitable crag was made.

By September, 1879, requisite government red tape was dispensed with and the lighthouse board was ready to begin construction. John R. Trewavas, a master mason from Portland, was chosen to head the construction crew. Trewavas went to the rock to make a thorough survey prior to the beginning of construction. As he jumped from the boat, he fell, and, as though it had been waiting for him, a wave sucked him off the rock and he sank. His body was

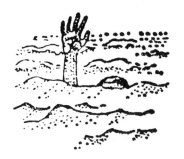

never recovered.

Near the end of October a force of eight workmen landed on the rock. Incredibly, they remained there through the winter, clinging to the rock through the violent, drenching storms, sheltering in a six by sixteen foot tent, and, through it all, drilling and blasting until, by May 1, 1880, they had removed about 29 feet from the rounded top of the rock and leveled a site large enough for the construction of

46

the lighthouse. The cornerstone was laid on June 22, 1880 and, on January 21, 1881, Tillamook Rock Lighthouse was operational.

The light, 80,000 candlepower, visible at sea for 18 miles, continued to shine until September, 1957, when the station was abandoned and the light replaced by a radar bouy. Like many other old lighthouses Terrible Tillie acquired a reputation of being haunted. James A. Gibbs, a former coastguardsman whose tour of duty included time on Tillamook Rock, told of his encounter with the ghost during his first midnight to morning watch at the light station. I found the following story in Gibbs' book, **Tillamook Light,** published by Binford and Mort of Portland in 1979.

I...suddenly found myself alone in the kitchen with four walls staring at me. I looked up at the old Regulator clock on the wall, which slowly ticked away the minutes. When the time came for my first rounds, I went outside into the cold, windy night to check the visibility. The atmosphere had cleared somewhat and a slight drizzle pricked my face. The roar of the sea was intense and all around was a black abyss, except when the probing beams of light from the beacon cut the darkness like a knife. For obvious reasons it was scary outside and I was glad to re-enter the fog signal house.

Continuing my rounds, I headed for the tower and began climbing the spiral staircase to check the light. As I ascended, my shoes clattered against the iron grates. The sounds called back at me, echoing off the tower walls. Just before I reached the watch room, I detected another unrelated noise, strange, haunting. Stopping in my tracks, I stood motionless. There it was again, a whispering moan, like one in pain.

"Oh, not again," thought I to myself...But this was different, and the utterance smacked of something human. Could one of the (other) keepers be trying to frighten me? "Oh, you foolish soul," thought I.

47

These old duffers had better things to do than go around playing ghost. Then I got to thinking of the conversation at the dinner table. Were there really such wraiths, I wondered, or were they only a figment of the imagination. I looked all around trying to figure out the source of those strange sounds but could draw no logical conclusion. Thus I hastily parted company with the unseen apparition, scurried into the watch room and then climbed the ladder to the lamp room.

....

I started back down the ladder, satisfied that all was well in the lamp room. Suddenly my thoughts were diverted back to the ghost in the tower. Sure enough, those same sounds were again audible in the same area. I was certain the three keepers were fast asleep at that hour, so it was just the spook and me. Then my eyes fell on a small door near the landing which I had evidently overlooked in surveying the lighthouse. Going back to the kitchen to get a flashlight, I returned to investigate. Could it be that the strange noises were coming from behind that door?

As if playing a role in a mystery movie, I automatically tiptoed toward the entrance. My hand reached for the handle. Timorous, I stepped back as it creaked open. Gathering my self-composure, I bolted inside. The air was dank and there was barely enough headroom to stand erect. As I flashed the light around, shadows played on the wall like hobgoblins around a witch's brew.

Finally I found a light bulb on the ceiling and pulled a protruding chain. At first it didn't respond, but finally a dim glow flooded the room which, as I was later to learn, had been created after the original metal lighthouse roof had been holed repeatedly by sea-thrown boulders. It was a storage area of sorts and a place to keep books sent from mainlanders who related to the lonely role of the lighthouse keepers. From the looks of the place nobody ever used it; cobwebs were everywhere. It was like the attic of an early American residence, with a littering of cast-

48

TILLAMOOK ROCK AND TILLAMOOK LIGHT in busier, happier days. When it closed in 1957, the rock became an almost-exclusive preserve for thousands of cormorants and murres, who turned it into a rookery and coated it with white droppings. The latest of a series of private owners may have brought the original ghost of the lighthouse some appropriately ghostly company, though. Since 1980 the old lighthouse has served as a depository for cremated human remains. (Photo courtesy of Oregon Historical Society)

49

offs. What a perfect home for the lighthouse ghost--and certainly a shadowy hideaway that needed future scrutiny. The floor creaked but the moaning sounds I heard in the tower were not in that room.

As the flashlight fell across the sagging bookshelves, I removed two volumes and returned to the more pleasant surroundings of the kitchen.

Making my entry in the log, I sat down to study the literary gems I had taken from the upper room. Blowing a collection of dust from the first, I discovered the auspicious title, **Tom Swift and the Motor Cycle**. Casting it aside, I picked up the other, which told about the old U. S. Lighthouse Service and some of its problems. I thumbed through to an article on the Navassa Lighthouse on a rock pile in the Caribbean and--wouldn't you know—on this night of all nights, there was an account of the supernatural. Inasmuch as it was an isolated seagirt lighthouse like Tillamook, my curiosity was naturally aroused and I read on. It went something like this:

The head keeper was an individual of 20 years' experience in lighthouses, quiet, practical, and certainly not a believer in supernatural things. He was chosen to handle the station after oppressive heat and miserable privation had delayed its completion until 1917. There was an indescribable something about that small island on the sea road to Panama (near Haiti and Cuba), rumor persisting that it was cursed, a holdover from the days when black laborers with white overlords off-loaded its guano resources. A mutiny among the workers had created a blood bath in which several were killed.

That first evening, the keeper-in-charge ascended the tower staircase (just as I had done **that** very night) and became conscious of the reverberating sound of his feet on the grates. After tending the light and while returning to the dwelling for coffee, he was aware of the camp, humid night, despite a clear, star-laden sky. Then he heard it—a loud, rhythmic wailing sound coming from outside, a sound resembling a man with a high-pitched voice accompanied by a shallow drum. Not believing in spooks and such trivia, despite having served in several lighthouses all claiming ghosts, he believed in a logical explanation for everything. Still, curiosity prompted the keeper to open the door and listen until the whistling wind finally drowned out the sound.

Nevertheless he took his lantern and inspected the area. Satisfied that no intruders were about, he started back. When he reached the dwelling, a loud cackling laugh from the sea pierced his ears. Believing it a strange combination of shrieking sea birds, he dismissed it from his mind, not sharing the experience with his assistant.

Two nights passed without consequence. On the third, it happened again. The keeper distinctly heard the same dull throbbing of the drum. While his assistant was winding the weights that turned the lens, he stole silently out into the night. Scurrying toward a clump of wild growth a short distance from the lighthouse, he hid himself from sight. Again the drums began beating, slowly and quietly at first, then gaining momentum and volume. The pulsating beat was mingled with the cry of birds and the incessant wind. Then came the same haunting voice that had startled him the first night, this time in a chant. The words sounded like, "Go 'way, white man, go ' way befo' too late!"

It was the call of one troubled, seemingly warning of impending doom. But how could this be? There was nobody else on the but the two attendants of the lighthouse. He wondered if the oppressive island possessed some strange mysticism. The tempo grew into a wild chant, the apparent warning continuing with greater rapidity as the drums grew ever louder.

While the listener crouched in the thick growth, the chanter's message, in broken English, seemed to be telling of the brutality heaped upon the blacks before the awful Navassa riot of yesteryear. Numbed by it all, the keeper made no attempt to capture his taunter nor was he able to see any clear image. Instead, each night when not on duty he returned to his secluded listening post to hear the chant. The entire episode smacked of voodoo, and this the keeper knew, but try as he would he could not resist the strange magnetic pull. The keeper became progressively morose and nervous. Alarmed by such behavior, the assistant watched his superior stare for hours on end at the vast sea, tapping his fingers on the table in the same tempo as the voodoo drums. Sometimes he was incoherent, neglecting his duties.

One day, as if in a trance, the troubled man came back to the lighthouse pale as a ghost, chanting a strange jargon and beating his chest in drum-like rhythm. He was stark mad. By running up distress flags, his frantic associate was able to attract a passing ship, but after signals were exchanged the vessel sailed away and it was two harrowing weeks before a lighthouse tender arrived off the island to remove the demented keeper.

The drums were then suddenly silenced and the voodoo chant was heard no more, nor was its originator, if any, ever found.

For a decade after the incident, the lighthouse service maintained personnel at the service, but few could stand the awful privation, the bloodsucking insects and fever. Voodoo rumors persisted all the while.

Finally, in 1929, the Lighthouse Service authorities threw in the sponge, admitting that Navassa was not fit for human habitation. The lighthouse was in turn automated at considerable expense and is still operated with occasional servicing from a buoy tender out of Miami.

It was almost ironic that I should come across such an article on my first night as a lighthouse keeper. I was careful, thereafter, not to take the ghost of Tillamook lightly.

It was one of the longest nights of my life, but finally out of the east a pale glow appeared over towering Tillamook Head, a giant monolith rising from the mainland beach a mile or so east of the rock. A sea mist hung low and the ocean had calmed

52

somewhat. Through the night I had imagined all kinds of things in the shadows and none of them seemed pleasant—clammy, wet, miserable things--the kind that make one wish for desert sunshine. In the days that followed, strange and ghostly visitations were seriously discussed and often considered as omens to be heeded. For some reason, lighthouses seem to spawn more than their share of ghostly tales and supernatural happenings.

My entry in the lighthouse log that morning was routine, for who would have believed my experiences of that night?

The Ghost
in Lithia Park

One night in 1975 some college students drove up a winding mountain road near Lithia Park in Ashland. Suddenly a misty blue apparition appeared in front of the car. As the car moved through the apparition, a coldness was felt by everyone in the car. Later that night one of the girls who had driven through the apparition awoke, hysterical, and was taken to the student health center for medication.

Some say that the girl in the car that night was the mirror image of another girl, who, nearly a century ago, was raped and murdered in the woods near Ashland. They believe that the apparition the students encountered that night was the dead girl's spirit, seeking to possess the spirit of her look-alike.

The Troll
of
Horny Chessman

Horny Chessman, believe it or not, is a campsite about 15 miles from Seaside, in an extremely rugged and isolated area of the Coast Range. Campers at Horny Chessman have occasionally seen a six-foot tall bear-like animal who walks on two legs, runs from humans, and wrecks fort-like campsites while the inhabitants are away. This creature may be Bigfoot or Sasquatch, but around Seaside he's known as the Troll of Horny Chessman.

The Ghost
of Charles Laughton

One of actor Charles Laughton's dreams was to play King Lear at the Oregon Shakespearean Theatre. Unfortunately, Laughton died shortly before he was to appear. When King Lear was first performed in Ashland after Laughton's death, an eerie sound was heard, passing through the audience and moving up onto the stage. Some say the sound was made by the ghost of Charles Laughton. They believe that Laughton's ghost haunts every performance of King Lear in Ashland.

Bandage Man

This business of hunting down Oregon's ghosts and monsters isn't always as easy as you might believe. For instance, consider what happened to me...

ONE NIGHT IN CANNON BEACH

"Ever hear of Bandage Man?" I asked the bartender in Bill's Tavern in Cannon Beach late one rainy evening last winter.

Grizzled heads turned all along the bar. A row of eyes fixed upon me and, in the sudden bar-room silence, I wondered if I'd said something wrong.

"Wasn't he a logger? Got hurt real bad or something?" The bartender, newly arrived from California, pushed a glass of beer across the bar to me.

"Naw. I'll tell you about Bandage Man." The old man was half the length of the bar from me and he said it so quietly that I barely heard. "C'mon, Maude."

He labored down from his perch on the barstool and slapped a skinny thigh to beckon the fat, old hound from where she slept at his feet. He carried his beer to a table near the door and crooked a finger at me as he settled into a comfortable wooden chair. Maude heaved herself under the table with a sigh. Thick rivulets of wind-driven rain rolled down the window as I crossed the smoky, wood-lined room.

The old man wore a blue stocking cap and a rust-colored down vest. A thick fringe of gray hair struggled from beneath the cap and a snowy white beard straggled down across his vest. He leaned comfortably back in the chair, clasped his weather-beaten hands across his stomach and looked square at me with the clearest blue eyes I've ever seen.

"See that newspaper article?" he asked, before I sat down, gesturing at the wall behind him to his right, where, camouflaged in a jumble of similar memorabilia, a yellowed clipping hung from rusty staples. "Injured Giant Disappears in Coastal Landslide," blared the headline.

"We all reckon," the old man said, glancing at the yellow clipping, "that that fellow became Bandage Man, because it wasn't more than two or three days later that people began to see him. Lots of people have seen him now, always late at night, usually a stormy night like tonight, and always, except the time he came visiting me and Maude, right there on that same stretch of road where he originally disappeared." He reached down and gave the old dog a little pat on the head. "Don't you worry, Maude," he said, "he ain't gonna get us."

Just then the door blew open and the wind blasted another person into our group.

"Evenin' boys," he said, peeling off a yellow tent of rain gear and tossing it over an empty chair in the corner. "Howdy, Emmet. Maude."

"Evenin' Armor." The old man responded without looking up as Maude wheezed and shifted her position slightly.

Armor was a wiry old leprechaun with a grin fixed permanently on his kindly, weatherbeaten face. His eyebrows were so thick that they knitted together over his nose and blended with the thick gray fringe that straggled around the hairless top of his strikingly shiny head. The effect was that of a large pink egg rising from a tousled gray nest. He drew a chair up to our table, settled back comfortably, and signalled the bartender for a pitcher of beer.

"What's goin' on, Emmet?"

"This fellow," the old man nodded at me, "wants to know about Bandage Man."

A glint crept into Armor's steely eyes. He leaned toward me, as if to tell me something he didn't want the others to hear. "Bandage man," he said quietly, with a sly glance down at Maude, "eats dogs."

I didn't know if he was serious, but the thought clearly made Maude uncomfortable. She gave Armor a rheumy glare and let out a low whine as she tried to slide under Emmet's chair. Armor settled back and took a long drink of his beer.

"I guess I was about the first person to see him after the accident." The speaker, easily the tallest man in the room, stretched out toward our table from his seat at the bar, his lanky, Levi-clad legs culminating in pointy-toed boots. A cowboy. He leaned against the bar, resting easily on his elbows, with a beer mug clasped between leathery hands across his belly. A shy smile revealed a mouthful of wide-spaced teeth. His was a long face, an appropriately horsey face, an honest and guileless face. This is not a man who will pull my leg, I thought.

As everyone in the tavern turned expectantly toward the cowboy, the wind began to moan through the cracks and gaps in the old wooden building. It shivered the tavern door and lashed the rain in great horizontal sheets against the window. The old building creaked under the onslaught and it was suddenly much colder inside. The lights flickered, then steadied, and the people in our little group seemed to draw closer together in the uncertain light. Maude groaned.

"Well," said the cowboy, slightly embarrassed at the attention, "course I didn't put it together at the time. Nobody did. Sure scared the hell out of me, though. Busted the back window in my pickup, too. Remember?"

Nods of assent, nervous sips, and a slight murmur said they remembered, but the cowboy reached for his beer mug and told the story anyway, for my benefit.

"It was a big mystery still, you know," he began, "what happened to the bandaged giant who disappeared from the ambulance. They'd finished the second search without finding any trace of him. But I wasn't thinking about that." He drained his mug and signalled the bartender for another.

"I was working in Seaside then, for a maintenance company. During the summer I run horses up here by Elk Creek, rent them to tourists, but during the winter, well, whatever comes along. We did floors and bathrooms and stuff, usually worked from about 5:00 to 11:30 or so. It was a Wednesday night. I remember because Wednesday was the day we did the Little Pig Market, and we'd finished a little later than usually that night, about ten minutes to twelve, I think. I was thinking I might stop in here for a beer before I went on home.

"Well, right up there, just past the turn-off from 101," he pointed north through the rain-streaked window, "I was cruisin' along, listening to the radio and trying to see the road through the rain. It was raining just about like tonight. I felt something, like a big gust of wind. The pickup just sort of lurched a little bit, kind of like the wind pushed me over on

58

the road a little."

Outside the tavern, the wind howled like a demon, shouldering its noisy way down the street, shaking buildings and rocking automobiles. It bashed the tavern door open, slammed it shut again three or four times in rapid succession, and blasted rain up against the front of the old building with a sound like wet buckshot falling on a tin roof. A shiver passed through the little crowd when the tavern lights flickered, went out, then came on again, permanently dimmed. The cowboy reached for his beer, took a long drink, then droned on through the storm.

"I drove on along and I started wondering about how much gas I had, because I meant to get some in Seaside, but I'd forgotten until just then. The instrument panel light on my pickup never worked, but I can see all the indicators by turning on the overhead light in the cab." He paused and took another sip from his beer mug.

"Well, sir," he looked at me and gave way to a little shudder, "still gives me a turn to remember it. I turned on the light in the cab. Turned out I had plenty of gas, but then, as I reached up to turn out the light, I heard this little noise. Sounded like something sort of scratching or rubbing on the outside of the cab. I glanced in the mirror and there was a mummy looking through the window at me." He shook his head as though he still had trouble believing what his eyes had told him that night. "I thought maybe the mirror was playing tricks on me, you know, rainy night and all, so I turned, like this." He turned and looked over his shoulder. "There he was, just a couple of inches away, riding along with me in the back of my pickup. When I turned around to look, we were almost cheek to cheek. He had his face pressed up against the back window of the pickup on the outside. When my face touched the window on the inside and I saw him there, I nearly died." He shuddered and shook his head.

"Then I thought, maybe it's a joke. Hallowe'en was gone but maybe one of these jokers," he gestured around the room, "was having himself a little laugh. I was pretty sure my pickup bed was empty when I left Seaside, though, and then, when I looked again, I knew it wasn't a joke. His eyes," he shivered again, drained his mug, "were just little holes in the bandages, with nothing inside. But his mouth, well, that was different. I could see lips, red lips kinda dripping something, maybe saliva or rain or blood, but it was night and..." Here he stopped for a long drink of the beer that appeared on the bar behind him. He wiped his mouth on the back of his arm and continued.

"Well, I figured I was safe. Windows rolled up, moving down the highway, him out there and me in the cab. Figured I'd just roll on into town and ease up here in front of the tavern where I knew there'd be a bunch of people and we'd all have a look at this guy. Just got that all figured out and was feeling kind of smug when KA-WHAM. It sounded like baseball hit the window just behind my head. He busted a little hole in it, then hit it again and the whole thing just caved in, big chunks of safety glass all over the cab. We were eyeball to eyeball, then.

"I could see the lights of the town coming up and I just held on and hoped I could get there. He grunted and growled and reached for me with a big bandaged hand. Got hold of my head, twisted me so I could hardly see where I was going. I couldn't get away, so I just tried to keep her on the road.

"Just as I got into town, he let go. There was, like a gust of wind, like happened when I figure he jumped into the pickup, and he was gone. I came sliding up here outside the tavern, drove on up over the curb and took out two parking meters before I got stopped. I was out of the pickup in a flash and busted in here all sick and shaky. Told these guys I needed help, to go look in my pickup. They all went out there, but he was gone. Slick as that, he disappeared. All he left behind was a hunk of that bandage, all bloody and smelling like rotten meat."

The wind howled and rattled the old building and Maude breathed a long sigh in a momentary stillness. The rain slackened a little. No one in our little group said anything for a few moments. The cowboy leaned back up against the bar and contemplated his beer.

Emmet finally broke the silence. "Now, there are lots of people who'll tell you they've seen Bandage Man," he said. "He's jumped on other pickups, station wagons, and even a sports car or two. A couple of times he's left broken windows and a shred or two of that awful bandage. He always attacks right about the same place, that stretch of road out toward 101, and he's always disappeared as soon as the car got to Cannon Beach. He's never seen during the day, either, but usually he pops up late on stormy nights. Like tonight."

"There are exceptions," the cowboy broke in.

"Yeah. I'm getting to that," Emmet assured him. "Two exceptions. One evening this fellow came in here and said he saw a mummy carry away a hitch-hiker. The fellow was scared to death and he'd already called the police, but of course they couldn't find anything. The man--he was from California, driving down the coast on his way home--said he saw this hitch-hiker, a young man, and he drove on by him a ways before he decided to give him a lift. He said that as he passed him he saw something odd behind him in the forest up there. Thought he saw a mummy in the trees, but it was almost dark and that's impossible anyway, so he didn't give it another thought. He'd never heard of Bandage Man.

"But then he stopped and backed up to give that young fellow a lift. When he looked in his rear view mirror, there was that mummy. Said it was about twice as big as the hitch-hiker. The mummy walked up behind that young fellow, mashed down on him with a big bandaged arm and the hitch-hiker folded up like a chair. Last the man from California saw, he said, Bandaged Man tucked that hitch-hiker under one arm like a loaf of bread and strolled off into the dark. Hitch-hikers avoid that stretch of road now, especially on stormy nights. Like tonight."

61

"People from around here," Armor said quietly, avoid that stretch of road any time after dark, whatever the weather."

"Yup," agreed the cowboy as another shiver danced up his spine. "Tell him what happened to you, Emmet."

"I was just fixin' to do that," Emmet said, placing his beer mug on the table and wiping the foam from his moustache. Maude groaned and the wind howled. The building shook, seemed to bend before the onslaught of the storm.

"Bandage Man hates Emmet," Armor said with a grin, "but he loves Maude." Maude groaned again and the wind momentarily held its sodden breath while Emmet began his story.

"I live up on the old dump road," he said, " and some people think Bandage Man lives up there somewhere, too. I don't know why they think that. I've never even seen him, except this one particular night I'm gonna tell you about.

"It was the winter of 1979. December. Coldest winter for forty years." Maude wheezed affirmatively from under the table. "Everything was froze up for miles up and down the coast. Icicles on all the cliffs, waterfalls frozen solid, ice on all the creeks, and, every night, when it got even colder, trees exploded like they'd been dynamited. It was so cold," he snuggled into his down vest to ward off the memory, "that spit froze before it hit the ground."

"Bear usually spend that part of the winter curled up in some hole, warm and cozy as can be. That's why it was real strange when dogs began to turn up missing. All over town, dogs were disappearing, but especially up there by where I live on the old dump road. It was like an epidemic. Old Maude here is the only dog for a mile in any direction from our house who survived that winter. Ain't that right, Maude?" Emmet reached down and scratched the old hound affectionately. "And she almost didn't make it."

Maude snored and wheezed in response as the wind roared around the tavern and the little group of listeners drew even closer together, like moths a-round the quiet flame of Emmet's drawl.

"Any other year we'd probably have figured that some old renegade bear was taking our dogs, but it was so cold that no bear would have missed out on hibernating that winter. At least, that's my theory. Besides," his eyes gleamed in the yellowish light, "there was other evidence. Those awful bandages. People were finding rotten bandages around after their dogs disappeared." He leaned forward in his chair and Maude became momentarily alert. "And footprints," Emmet continued, "we found only human footprints. Big ones."

"Then there was poor old Madge," he said sadly, pulling an enormous red handkerchief from his back pocket and dabbing gently at the corners of his eyes. Maude groaned again, louder than before.

"Madge was Maude's best friend, our neighbor up there by the dump for years. They were puppies together." Emmet blew his nose and took another swipe at his eyes. "About the second or third day of the deep freeze, Maude and I were out for a walk when we found her body. Or what was left of her body. It was terrible. She was ripped apart and al-most all eaten up. All that was left was some bones and a few shreds of her hide. Even her head was gone. There was human tooth marks in what was left, and right near where we found her was one of those stinking bandages."

Emmet sat back and took a long drink of his beer. Maude groaned ever so sadly and the wind re-newed its attack on the old building, bashing the tav-ern door open and slamming it shut, admitting great wet gusts of the storm.

"Well," Emmet continued, his composure re-gained, "the story got round that Bandage Man was eating the dogs. I believed it. We got together and went looking for him. But, of course, we couldn't find him."

He paused for a long drink. Then, with a deep sigh: "He found us. Maude and me."

The wind whistled around the building and Maude groaned, loud this time, and barked a little whimpering kind of a bark as she tried to shove herself farther under Emmet's chair. The lights flickered, dimmed again, and stayed there. Outside, something crashed, maybe a garbage can blown over in the gale. I glanced toward the rain-swept window and thought I caught a glimpse of someone or something moving past.

"It was a lot colder than tonight," Emmet continued, "but it was windy, just like now. Howling and roaring around our house, but we were snug as two bugs in a rug. I like nights like that. Built a big fire in the stove and we just settled back with the newspaper. Now Maude, she's not much of a watchdog, but I'd noticed that she was mighty nervous that night. I thought maybe she was just upset about Madge, but she was moaning and wheezing and barking a little, like she's been doing tonight. Didn't think anything of it, though."

Maude barked again, louder this time. Something, lightning, maybe, flashed out in the rain, illuminating the street for an instant. The rain drummed louder and louder on the old building.

"I'd just got comfortable," Emmet said, "and I was sitting there listening to the wind. Maude was mighty nervous. She was looking right at the window, not three feet from where we sat, growling and barking. Not like her at all. I said, 'Quiet, Maude,' then looked at the window to see what she was barking at."

Maude was barking louder now, at the rain-streaked tavern window.

"Well, sir," Emmet paused, shook his head, "I looked out that window smack at that mummy. Yessir. He was standing right there on my front porch, looking at me and Maude." Emmet took a long drink of his beer, and the wind, redoubling its attack on the tavern, bashed the old wooden door open once again.

"When he saw me looking at him that window

64

just exploded. He smacked with one of those big bandaged paws and busted it all over the room. Glass everywhere. He leaned through the hole and reached for Maude. He got his hand on her, but she was fighting like crazy, biting and tearing those rags. That mummy was having a time hanging on to her. Hush, Maude."

The old dog was barking frantically now, eyes fixed on the tavern window and toenails flailing the floor as she tried to back farther under Emmet's chair. Emmet's eyes bulged and his nostrils flared and he moved forward to the edge of his chair.

"I jumped up out of my chair and tripped, or he tripped me. Not sure which. I was trying to get my shotgun. When I looked back he'd hooked Maude and it looked like he was gonna drag her out the window. She was fighting like mad, though, weren't you, girl?" He leaned down and patted the top of her head. Maude was growling quietly now, her eyes still fixed on the tavern window. "Hush, girl. He ain't gonna get us."

The storm worked its way to a new peak now. The whole building quivered around us, and the lights dropped another notch.

"I got across the room on my knees, grabbed that gun and let him have it." Emmet stood and shouted, levelling an imaginary shotgun at the far end of the tavern. "Never said nothing. Just shot. BLAM. Couldn't miss at that range. Blew a hole right through him."

Maude growled and barked even louder now, and renewed her effort to back under Emmet's chair. I glanced toward the window as the old man paused, saw nothing but more rain and perhaps a flash of light. The old man sat down again.

"He dropped Maude and looked at me for a second. Then he grabbed Maude again and I let him have the other barrel. BLAM. Two great big holes, but there didn't seem to be anything inside. He turned around and ran off toward the old dump, loose ends of bandages flapping about in the wind. Never seen him since."

Maude was going crazy now, and so was the storm. The old dog growled and scratched and barked, her eyes glued to the wood frame window. The wind raged against the old building, bashing the door open once again.

The lights in the old tavern flickered again and went out. Darkness.

Outside in the storm, another flash of light blared through the dark, illuminating the rain-swept street and, in the window, a ghastly silhouette.

The old tavern window caved in with a terrible crash. A powerful smell of rotten meat rode into the tavern on the storm. The grisly figure lurched through the opening and groped in the darkness toward Maude and Emmet. Tables, chairs, beer mugs and bodies crashed to the floor as the members of our little group dived apart, each of us scrambling to get as far as possible from the foul-smelling monster.

Maude's fierce growl rose quickly in the darkness to a terrified shriek, then subsided to a gurgle. Then, a sound like the breaking of a tree limb and she was quiet. Blows fell on something, then the grim silhouette passed through the opening into the storm.

Pacific Power and Light Company said later that the lights were out for less than five minutes in Cannon Beach that night, but to us it seemed like five hours. When power was restored we crawled from our hiding places and peered sheepishly at one another.

Maude was gone. Emmet was gone. Only a little patch of blood and a couple of clumps of dog hair suggested they'd ever been more than figments in a dream. Also gone, though we didn't discover it till later, was the yellowed newspaper clipping. On a glass sliver in the window frame hung a shred of blood-stained, rotten bandage.

An ear that could have been Maude's turned up on the sidewalk at the north end of Cannon Beach a couple of days after the storm, but no other trace of Maude or Emmet has been found. Bandage Man was

66

never captured.

During the very next storm, though, perhaps a week later, a shaken motorist stumbled frantically out of the darkness into Bill's Tavern, claiming that a giant mummy had attacked his car near the Highway 101 turnoff.

Everyone told him he was crazy.

The Ghost
in
Battery Russell

If you every go out to Battery Russell (in Fort Stevens near Astoria) at night, you're likely to hear the clanking of chains as the ghost of Battery Russell makes his nightly rounds. Some say he comes clanking down the old deserted walkways, almost impossible to see behind his flashlight and then, when he's almost upon you, he disappears.

Ghost Ship
on the
Columbia Bar

May 4, 1880, was a terrible day at the mouth of the Columbia. The spring salmon season, shortened by striking fishermen at its beginning, was finally underway, and pressure to make the remaining time as profitable as possible was immense. In spite of threatening weather, the entrance to the Columbia River was crowded with fishermen in sailing gill net boats.

The storm came quickly, a howling gale out of the southwest that turned the Columbia bar into a roaring mass of breakers. Fishermen strained to haul in their nets and and sail to safety, but many were drawn irresistably into the breakers. The frail fishing boats were tossed about like toys and fishermen were heaved like dolls into the raging surf. Some fishermen drowned when they became entangled in their own nets. Some just vanished, but others managed to cling to their overturned boats until they were rescued or drifted to shore hours later.

C. Christianson told **The Daily Oregonian** on May 7, 1880, "My boat was at anchor when a very heavy sea came and upset her almost alongside of James Hainson's boat. She righted immediately. My boat filled. Hainson then got in the boat, but I was entangled in the net and I could not get in until a breaker threw me in. Hainson asked me if I should cut the painter. I said yes, and then we drifted opposite Megler's station, shouting for help. Hainson said we can never be saved. A few minutes after he commenced crying. I said don't get discouraged; while there is life there is hope. I think we will be all right, as we were now drifting very fast. A moment after a breaker came and threw me out of the boat almost on the beach. After a struggle in the breakers

68

I succeeded in reaching land. I was in the water from 6 P. M., clinging to the boat, to 2 A. M. Hainson had lashed himself to the boat and died there, as his body was seen lying over the bow of the boat, stiff and rigid."

John M. Neal, a boatpuller, "...drifted with net for about four hours or more; wind increased to a lively gale; sea was breaking very heavily; saw several boats capsize, one in particular; that was a little astern of us, drifting; turned over when only one of the men appeared to have been able to scramble on to the keel as the breakers were running very high and the wind was still increasing. We were under the necessity of letting go our net or else lose our lives, so we let go and pulled towards the boat spoken of to try and pick the men up, but the heavy sea prevented; so we had the misery of seeing the poor fellows perish about two or three boat's length from us..."

Later references to the storm of May 4, 1880, call it the worst tragedy ever on the river and put the toll of lives lost at "some 200 Columbia River fishermen," (Oregonian, January 19, 1969). **The Daily Astorian** of May 8, 1880, however, says: "From the best sources that we have been able to obtain information, the losses of life by the late storm on this bay, foots up to nineteen men."

The **Daily Oregonian** (May 6, 1880) says, "At one time it was reported that ten men were known to be lost, but the reports have been so conflicting that we know not for a certainty whether any lives were lost or not..." The correspondent for the **Daily Oregonian** lays the blame for loss of life and property partly on fishermen who know better but intentionally fish too near the breakers and, quoting "Those who ought to know", on that old demon, whisky. The whisky charge was later denied by the fishermen, defended by the correspondent from **The Daily Oregonian,** and denounced in **The Daily Astorian.** By May 7, 1880, **The Daily Oregonian** had compiled enough information to estimate "...that not less than 25 lives have been lost and probably 10 to 15 boats and nets."

One fishing boat, however, was unaffected by the gale. It sailed serenely through the wreckage of the fishing fleet, and past the astonished fishermen, many of whom were floating in the treacherous water or clinging precariously to the bottoms of their capsized fishing boats. Though seen by several survivors of the May 4 storm, it was recognized by none. The ghost boat of the Columbia Bar was never seen again.

The Phantom Bugler

Around Forest Grove they still talk about the Phantom Bugler. He was a huge man, the old bugler. Folks around Forest Grove would see him in the old days, striding through the woods, the bugle slung around his shoulders on a wide leather strap.

His bugle was bigger than an ordinary bugle. The sound it made was different, lower, than the usual music made by a bugle, and those who heard it were apt to confuse it with the sound of the wind in the trees. No one ever heard it, though, unless they were alone in the woods. Then, like a low whisper, it would come to them and, almost like magic, the old bugler would appear on their path.

The old bugler was attacked one day by a cougar. In the course of a terrific fight, he managed to kill the cougar, using his only weapon, the bugle. After the fight, he lay on the path, so weakened by loss of blood that he lapsed into unconsciousness. For two days and two nights he lay in the woods, drifting in and out of consciousness, until he regained enough strength to drag himself back to his tiny cabin.

Since that day, only one man has seen the old bugler and lived to tell about it. He was walking through the woods when he heard a low whistling

70

sound. Thinking it was the wind, he just kept walking. Suddenly, the old bugler appeared, blocking the path. The old man's face was lined with scars, apparently from the fight with the cougar, and he looked mad. He raised the bugle slowly, and then, to the horror of the man from Forest Grove, lunged and swung the bugle at the man's head with force enough to crush his skull. The man ducked and ran, and kept running until he was out of the woods.

This happened nearly 70 years ago, but every few years, some say, someone is found in the woods near Forest Grove with his or her head split open, the wound possibly caused by a blow from an oversized bugle, the work, some say, of the Phantom Bugler.

The Ghost of the John Day Fording

Long ago, in the days before bridges crossed Oregon's rivers, Daniel Leonard and his wife Mary ran a ferry and a hotel just east of Wasco, where the Oregon Trail crossed the John Day River. Daniel and Mary were said to have murdered several hotel patrons for their gold and money, which they buried carefully near the hotel.

After several years at the John Day Crossing, an argument broke out between the two. Mary killed her husband. She was tried, convicted of murder, and sentenced to prison.

Early in this century Mary Leonard, by then an old woman with long, white hair and a "wild appearance", was released from the penitentiary. She returned to the John Day crossing and enlisted the aid of a local farmer in locating her buried treasure. "A

71

light will appear at midnight," Mrs. Leonard told the farmer, "to guide us to the money." Night after night they searched, but to no avail. Mary Leonard eventually gave up and was never seen in that area again.

In later years, people who lived at the stage station told of seeing the ghost of an old woman roaming the house. The ghost had long white hair, wore a long, flowing dress, and passed with ease through walls and closed doors. When spoken to, the ghost vanished.

The old stage station was torn down, probably sometime in the 1950's, but the ghost of Mary Leonard, some say, still haunts the river bank, searching for her ill-gotten treasure.

Lemures
in Mount Ashland

Some say that lemures (ghosts) who possess scientific powers that border on being magical live in a city inside Mount Ashland. These lemures are said to have hollowed their city out of the mountain's interior, using powerful vibrations produced by a bell-like instrument. Relics of lemurian civilization are said to have been found on Table Rock in Jackson County.

The Ghost
in the
Umatilla County Library

Ruth, an old-time Pendleton librarian, was des-
pondent over a failed love affair when she decided to
end her misery in the basement of the Umatilla County Library. Why she chose lye and how she could sit
there and quietly eat the whole thing, no one seems
to know. She was found, writhing in agony, and rushed to St. Anthony's Hospital, where she died.

Since that time, strange things have happened in
the library. Books fall from shelves, footsteps are

heard when no one is there, windows open themselves, and, when the lights go out at night, the
building creaks mysteriously as the librarians rush
toward the door.

Ruth's ghost, some say, still lurks in the stacks
at the Umatilla County Library. (Rainy Day Press
Photo)

Lavender

When I heard the story of the girl in the lavender dress I didn't know that it was a classic American ghost story, that Lavender had appeared and disappeared in a variety of similar places all around the
country. Still, it's hard for me to believe that Lavender didn't actually live--and die--in that rolling hill
country northeast of Pendleton, or that, if I went
back today, the tombstone with "Jean Louise" letter-
ed on its front wouldn't still be there, exactly as it
is in the story.

I first heard the story of the girl in the lavender dress while lying around the bunkhouse on the
Irvin Mann Ranch, swapping stories with other young
harvest workers. I never knew the young men in the
story, but I once knew someone who did. The house
where Lavender lived, now deserted, still stands,
exactly as described in the story. I've been there and
I could lead you there today.

The Girl in the Lavender Dress

It was unusually cool for early summer, pea
harvest time in the rolling fields northeast of Pendleton. A thunderstorm drenched the area the previous
night, turning dusty pea fields into bogs of slippery,
sucking mud. The rains continued throughout the day.

For Rick MaHane and David Nelson and the
other young men who drove for the Mann Ranch, the
whole day had been a struggle. From six o'clock in

74

the morning until six o'clock in the evening they flogged their old Internationals and GMC's through the muck from loader to viner and back again. The big machines roared and bounced, slipped and slid, and, too often, sank to the hubs, stuck.

Stuck. The Cat flails across the mud to the rescue. The Cat driver, top man in the ranch hand pecking order, hates to get wet. The truck driver, on his knees in the rain, mud flowing over the tops of his boots, wrestles the heavy chain behind the Cat, attaches it to the truck, genuflects appropriately. The Cat chugs ahead. Sssuck. Thwop. The old International lunges forward, liberated. The truck driver, again on his knees in the mud, wrestles the chain back, stows it properly on the mammoth tractor. Another genuflection and the Cat is off across the soggy field to rescue another truck. The peas are ready. The harvest must go on. Wet, cold, tired, muddy. It was not a good day for pea truck drivers.

But the good times were coming. The work day behind them, a six-pack on the seat between them, MaHane and Nelson were off to the dance. They were driving the backroads, beer-drinking roads, down to Thorn Hollow, along the Umatilla River through the reservation to Mission and then to Pendleton.

Before they'd gone far they were surprised by the sight of a lovely girl standing at the roadside. She smiled through the rain and beckoned the car to stop. Mahane slammed on the brakes.

"Can we help you?" The girl wore a lavender party dress, the skirt of which nearly brushed the muddy ground. The bodice of the lavender dress was spangled with little glistening jewels sewn in a pattern of tiny leaves. Hair the color of an August wheat field flowed radiantly across her shoulders and down her back. She wore no jacket, but did not appear uncomfortable in the rain.

"I wonder if you could give me a ride into town," she answered.

She explained, as they drove into Pendleton, that she lived with her mother just over the hill in a small house in an oak grove in the center of the vast field beside which they had picked her up.

MaHane remembered the house. He saw it a week or so earlier when the Mann Ranch crew harvested that field, and had supposed it to be deserted.

She planned to go to Pendleton with a friend, she said, but, at the last minute, the friend could not go, so she resorted to the unsual steps that gained her the ride with MaHane and Nelson. Coincidentally, she also intended to attend the dance at the Pendleton Armory. They decided to go together.

The night was a sparkling success. The happy threesome stayed late at the dance, the young men oblivious to the threat of another day of hard, muddy work approaching with the dawn. The girl--Lavender was her name--danced tirelessly with both Nelson and MaHane, but, as the night wore on, it became obvious that MaHane was her favorite. Nelson graciously faded away and MaHane held Lavender tightly in his arms through the last, slow tunes that ended the evening.

As the three young people crossed the parking lot arm in arm after the dance, rain began to fall once again. MaHane insisted that Lavender wear his rain jacket, and he placed it around her shoulders.

They drove back to the ranch the way they had come, out through Mission, along the river to Thorn Hollow, then up the back roads toward Adams. MaHane turned his car through the gap in the fence where they had met Lavender earlier in the evening. The car bounced and slid along the rough, little-used track that led across the field. A little thatch of forest and rocks stood hidden in the gully about half a mile from the road. The lights cut through the rain and darkness and Lavender pointed out the path that led to her house.

The car easily navigated the overgrown trail, and they soon pulled up in front of a little white house that stood between two huge oak trees. Lavender was out of the car and up the three steps to the porch in a flash. She turned at the door and flashed a dazzling smile, and then, with a little wave, disappeared inside, leaving her two escorts in stunned silence in the car.

It wasn't until they pulled into the parking lot near the bunkhouse at the Mann Ranch that MaHane realized Lavender had forgotten to return his jacket.

"Good," he thought. "That gives us an excuse to see her tomorrow."

The rain tapered off during the following day. By the end of the work day the solid cloud cover was broken. When the two young men pulled up in front of the tumbledown white house, the sun broke through and bathed the vast pea fields and the little oak grove in a warm red glow.

The house looked even smaller, the flanking oak trees even larger, in the soft evening light. One of the support posts was gone and a moss-covered roof teetered over the sagging porch. A shattered pane in the window to the right of the door was patched with a yellowed shred of cardboard. MaHane's initial impression that the house was deserted came back to him as he walked up the three rotting steps to the porch.

A tattered gray curtain hung over the window in the upper half of the old wooden door. Thin glass rattled loosely with Nelson's light knock, and the door sagged open with a rusty squeak. A withered woman in a raggedy gray dress materialized from the darkness inside the house.

"Can I help you?" she asked, baring toothless gums in an attempt to smile.

Mahane explained that they had come to see Lavender.

"Are you old friends of hers?" the old woman asked.

"Uh, yes, ma'am," Nelson responded quickly, fearing that the old lady might not understand the circumstances under which their relationship had blossomed the previous night.

"Well, you must not have heard. She's dead," the old woman told them sadly. "Died ten years ago."

Shocked, the two young men explained that the girl they sought couldn't be dead, that they'd been with her just the previous night. They described the girl and told the old woman of the lavender party dress. "She was wearing my jacket when we brought her here," MaHane told her.

"That was my Lavender," the old woman insisted. "No one else like that ever lived here. Dead ten years. Her real name was Jean Louise, but we called her Lavender because it was her favorite color. She liked that nickname. She was buried in a lavender dress like the one you described."

The old woman then led the horrified pair to the rear of the house. A small family graveyard, nearly overgrown with grass and brambles, lay among the oaks.

"There." She pointed to a moss-covered tombstone. The lettering, "Jean Louise", was visible through the moss, as was the date, exactly ten years previous. The jacket Rick MaHane had placed around Lavender's shoulders the night before lay neatly folded on top of the tombstone.

Hot Lake
Hotel

HOT LAKE was a stagecoach stop before the spooky old brick building now standing on the lakeshore was built in 1907. The great expectations indicated by this sign are apparently on hold at present. (Rainy Day Press Photo)

"Emerging from the chain of Blue Mountains, they descended upon a vast plain, almost a dead level, sixty miles in circumference, of excellent soil, with fine streams meandering through it in every direction, their courses marked out in the wide landscape by serpentine lines of cotton-wood trees, and willows, which fringed their banks, and afforded sustenance to great numbers of beavers and otters.

"In traversing this plain, they passed, close to the skirts of the hills, a great pool of water, three hundred yards in circumference, fed by a sulphur spring, about ten feet in diameter, boiling up in one corner. The vapor from this pool was extremely noisome, and tainted the air for a considerable distance. The place was much frequented by elk, which were found in considerable numbers in the adjacent mountains, and their horns, shed in the spring time, were strewed in every direction around the pond."

Washington Irving
Astoria
Published in 1836

"Walter Pierce, who was later to become governor of Oregon and member of Congress, built the brick hotel building, with 22-inch walls, in 1907. Its 105 rooms are heated with spring water which leaves the ground at a temperature of 208.

In its heyday the Hot Lake resort employed 175 and served 2000 to 3000 meals daily. Every train stopped at its roofed but unsided station to drop or pick up health-seekers or vacationists, who flocked to the Grande Ronde from as far east as Omaha..."

Spokesman Review
November 6, 1949

Today Hot Lake Hotel is a decrepit old wreck, light years from its heyday. Shrouded behind a gauze-like curtain of steam and mist, the old brick building stands against the base of a hill in the Grande Ronde Valley, midway between Union and La Grande. Signs posted around the hotel hint that a visit might not be good for your health or safety, and the building itself has an aspect of foreboding, a vacant, unfriendly look that does not bid the traveler welcome. But wait. Look again. Let your imagination run back a few years...

HOT LAKE HOTEL. Mist still rises from the restful, healing waters. (Rainy Day Press Photo)

Though its shoreline has been considerably modified since the coming of the white man, the lake has been here for hundreds, perhaps thousands, of years. Before even the Indian came to the Grand Ronde Valley, Hot Lake was the centerpiece in a vast feeding ground for an immense variety of wildlife. Before the white man entered the valley, Indians established a neutral area at Hot Lake, so members of different tribes could come in peace and safety to enjoy the soothing waters. Later, as tension between the white man and the Indian mounted, Hot Lake was a place of peaceful intercourse between the races. Lewis and Clark camped near Hot Lake, and fur traders sent from the east by John Jacob Astor celebrated New Year's Day, 1812, in the same vicinity, with a "...sumptuous new-year's banquet of dog's-meat and horse-flesh".

Early in this century, the "Mayo Clinic of the West" was born in a huge brick building on the lakeshore, and well-to-do people came from all over the country to "take the cure" for ailments as diverse as alcoholism and syphilis. A huge gabled building stretched along the lakeshore to the right of the gaunt old brick building, forming one side of an elegant, tree-shaded avenue where Daisy Buchanan might have felt right at home.

I first heard about the ghosts at Hot Lake Hotel several years ago from the librarian in the Union City Library. "Hot Lake Hotel is haunted," she told me. At that time rehabilitation work was being done on the hotel. Her husband was among the workmen. "He won't work on the third floor any more," she told me. "Almost no one will."

Shortly after that trip to Union I put this book aside to work on other projects. In August, 1983, I was in Union again and I called Dr. Ty Griffith of La Grande, one of the owners of Hot Lake Hotel, to ask permission to enter the grounds and photograph the hotel. When I told him of my proposed book, Dr. Griffith refused to allow me to enter the hotel grounds, saying over and over "Hot Lake Hotel is not a haunted house. Did know that?"

The elegant gabled building is gone, burned in a raging fire in 1934. The brick building and a few smaller buildings remain and mist still rises from the restful, healing, waters, but the parking lot, once full of glistening Packards, Hudsons and Cadillacs, is empty. The old building is ugly now, just an eyesore perched on the edge of a mineral lake at the base of a treeless hill. The gaunt old hotel looks neglected, unkempt, unfriendly, haunted.

Maybe Dr. Griffith is right: "Hot Lake Hotel is not a haunted house..." On the other hand, there was never a building anywhere that looked more haunted than Hot Lake Hotel does today, and there are those, as the following story (From the **La Grande Observer**, October 27, 1977) attests, who believe that, indeed, there are ghosts at Hot Lake Hotel.

HOT LAKE RESORT. The train stopped each day, bringing vacationers from all over the world. (Photo Courtesy of Oregon Historical Society)

ARE THERE
GHOSTS AT HOT LAKE?

By Dick Cockle

This time of year, the cold autumn winds, mists and cavernous buildings of Hot Lake Resort give it an air that is, well--haunting.

Sequestered beside a thermal hot lake, seven miles southeast of La Grande, Hot Lake Resort has been regarded for three years as one of the finest eating places in the Grande Ronde Valley. But among those who know it well, it has another, stranger reputation.

Overnight guests there have reported hearing sounds of footfalls from the resort's upper chambers, ghostly melodies from a distant piano -- and, sometimes, screams.

Dave and Donna Pattee, who operated a restaurant and hotel on the first floor until this month, say the resort's early tenants occasionally seem to stir when the daytime guests leave.

83

"My mother lived there," Donna Pattee says, indicating a first-floor apartment. "That was when we first moved to Hot Lake. She said that at night people walked up and down the hallways. She could also hear people on the second floor."

Her mother was alone in the building when the nighttime sounds occurred. The elderly woman never ventured outside her room or upstairs after dark.

Strains from a piano on the empty third floor were sometimes heard by a waitress who lived alone for a short time in the building, says Mrs. Pattee. And an accountant friend who stayed in a first-floor apartment was disturbed by the ghostly goings-on, according to Dave Pattee.

"They used to hear people up there having parties, and voices and laughter," he says.

Hot Lake Resort has a checkered history. The first paying guests stayed at a small hotel there in 1851, when the road beside the resort was still the Oregon Trail. The area was transformed into a resort in the 1890s.

The current brick structure at Hot Lake is about 70 years old, all that remained after a fire in the 1930s destroyed the main resort.

"The beautiful part burned," says Donna Pattee. "When it was there, they had a big ballroom and a library. They had big birdcages with parrots in them and great big Boston firs all over. They said it was just beautiful.

Hot Lake at that time was both a resort and a hospital. Its 205-degree mineral springs were considered salubrious for the treatment of arthritis, tuberculosis, alcoholism and syphilis.

Operated by Dr. W. T. Phy, "they referred to it as the Mayo Clinic of the West," Donna Pattee says. "In the medical profession, he was beyond his years. He was a genius."

When the Pattees took over the resort three years ago, part of the upper floors were being used as a rest home. It was after the rest home closed that the stories of ghosts began to be told.

The person who best knows the ghosts of Hot Lake Resort is Richard Owens, 27, a caretaker who lived more than a year on the second floor. He left six months ago and now resides in Hermiston.

Owens claims he often heard a piano in a third floor room play at night when the building was empty.

THE END OF ELEGANCE. Fire destroyed about half of Hot Lake Resort on May 8, 1934. (Photo Courtesy of Oregon Historical Society)

"Sometimes it would just play for five minutes. Sometime it would play for a while. After you lived out there as long as I did, you don't pay any attention to it. You don't want to pay any attention to it," he says.

But the piano didn't bother Owens as much as the screams.

"My room was directly under the old surgery room, and you'd hear it real plain. There's a woman that screams up there. It sounds like somebody's got her tied up or something."

There were other things, too.

"I would put stuff in certain places and it would get moved," Owens says.

"When I'd go up to the third floor, I would always push the piano chair under the piano. But when I'd get back, the piano chair would be out in the middle of the room, and it's a big room. Inside the piano chair was some sheet music, and once in a while that music would be out on the piano.

"There's just no way that prowlers or anything are going to do that," Owens says. "Besides, they just couldn't get in. That third floor is locked up real tight.

"Things would get out of locked rooms. I had some wheelchairs get out of a locked room once, and the room was still locked," he adds.

Occasionally Owens would hear footfalls on a wheelchair ramp that links the first and second floors. "You can hear the footfalls coming right up the ramp. You can jerk the door open and there won't be a soul there," he says.

The third floor frightened Owens, particularly when he had to go up there on rainy nights to empty water buckets under a leak.

"It would be pitch dark, because the light bulbs burned out or the electricity was off. That was real scary. It took a lot to get me to go down them dark hallways. That's a long way and I didn't like doing it at all, but it had to be done.

"I wouldn't sleep a night on the third floor. I'm sure they wouldn't bother me, but there's just some things I don't want to know about," Owens says.

Donna Pattee doesn't believe in ghosts. But she admits that the old building disturbs her. For instance, there are three rocking chairs on the third floor, the seats of which never seem to get dusty. She says it's as if somebody or something sits in them...

Owens called Mrs. Pattee's attention to the ab-

HOT LAKE TODAY. No vacancy--at least for humans. (Rainy Day Press Photo)

sence of dust on the rockers. She was trying to verify it for herself by checking them regularly when she discovered the chairs also had a tendency to move about in the room when nobody was there.

"I placed them in a certain way out of curiosity, and I went back later and they were moved," she says.

Whatever prowls the hallways and empty corridors of the old building apparently prefers the darkness.

"I would leave the light on in one of the rooms, so if I had to go up there it wouldn't be in total darkness, because it is dark up there," Donna Pattee

87

says. "And I'd go up there and they'd be off."

A year ago, the Pattees attempted to bring an end to the nocturnal piano playing and dress up the restaurant's dining room. They moved the ancient piano downstairs from the third floor.

"The night that we moved it down, there was a kind of restlessness on the third floor. You just heard a lot of creaking and groaning," recalls Owens.

The piano does indeed ornament the dining room. But the move didn't halt the strange playing.

The Pattees' 26-year-old son David was talking to friends about (?) feet from the dining room one night after the restaurant closed when the Pattees claim the piano began to play. The dining room was empty.

"We just let it play," says Owens, who was there when that happened. "it sounded like maybe how a kid would play, or like an older person in agony."

Before moving to Hot Lake, Owens says he didn't pay much attention to ghost stories. He does now.

"I'd say if a person lived in there for a month, they would come out believing in spirits," he says.

"There could be a logical explanation. The wind blows a lot out there. Maybe the wind could make it sound like a woman's screams, but I've heard that when there was no wind. There's definitely something up on the third floor as far as I'm concerned. I was never the adventurous type, so I never investigated to see what it was."

Dave Pattee takes a more cavalier attitude toward Hot Lake's ghosts.

"Oh, I think a lot of people have expired before their time in this building -- you bet they did. You can't have a building of this age and this history without a ghost or two. It wouldn't be right," he says with a laugh.

Usually Donna Pattee agrees: "I think it's just a lot of nervous tension from a big old building with lots of shadows and creaks."

But there are times when she's not so sure.

"I don't believe... Well, sometimes I really wonder, " she says. "I would say I get a queasy feeling upstairs. I don't enjoy going up there alone at night."

The Monster
in
Wallowa Lake

My father saw the monster in Wallowa Lake.

He was a child at the time, fishing from the bank. From his description, I've always pictured it as a huge snake with a head like a Chinese dragon, a regular medieval sea serpent, rippling across the surface of the lake, pausing momentarily to look at the little fisherman on the shore and then vanishing serenely into the lake.

Irene Wiggins saw it, too.

"I've seen the darn thing a couple of times," said Mrs. Wiggins, who has owned the lodge at Wallowa Lake since 1945. She was on horseback, on the moraine which forms the east side of Wallowa Lake, when she saw it. "Its head was a big, black thing, like a hog's head," she said, estimating its weight at "several hundred pounds". The monster swam across the lake, away from her, bobbed up and down a few times, and then, near the far shore, disappeared. "I wished I had a camera," she said.

The story of the Wallowa Lake monster originated with the Nez Perce Indians, who roamed the northeastern corner of Oregon and much of what is now southeast Washington, Idaho, and Montana, and who made their summer home on the shores of Wallowa Lake before the white man arrived in Oregon. George A. Waggoner heard one version of the story from Chief Joseph while passing through the Wallowa country in the 1860s. He included it in his book, **Stories of Old Oregon,** published in 1905 by the Statesman Publishing Company in 1905 in Salem:

A Legend of Wallowa Lake.

At Boise City I purchased a couple of mule teams of eight mules each, and proceeded on the way to Wallula for a load of freight. As my mules had come across the plains that season, I concluded to stop in Grande Ronde Valley, where the grass was good, and let them recruit.

I made camp about ten miles down the valley from where the old immigrant road enters it, and to employ the time, went elk hunting. Three of us in the party, we rode about twenty miles north and camped on the mountain near Wallowa Valley. The next morning, near our camp, we met six Wallowa Indians going after a band of elk they had seen the evening before near our camp. We accepted their invitation to go with them. One of them was a young chief named Joseph, afterwards to cause much trouble as the leader of an insurrection against the whites in 1878, and generally known as the Nez Perce War, although few Nez Perce Indians were in the outbreak. Chief Joseph was quite an intelligent Indian, and was recognized then as a leader among his people. He said we must observe great caution in approaching the elk, and be sure to kill all we wanted first, for elk, when frightened, will travel ten or twelve miles before they stop, and then will keep pickets out behind and be on the lookout for several days.

We kept under cover as much as possible, and approached cautiously until, emerging from a strip of timber, we were within thirty yards of the game we sought. All unconscious of our presence, they were taking their ease, about forty of them. Some were feeding, some were lying down, and one old fellow nearest us appeared to be asleep standing on his feet. His eyes were closed and he lazily flapped his long ears to drive away the gnats that hummed about him. Joseph gave the signal by raising his rifle, and nine shots rang out almost as one report. Four elk dropped in their tracks, and the rest, instead of running away, turned startled eyes upon us and stood still. We had muzzle loading rifles and nine powder horns were raised at once for another charge of powder. Before we were ready to fire again the herd started to run; As they plunged down the hill we gave them another volley. When it was all over, we had thirteen fat elk for our morning's work.

The Indians were delighted, and returned to their village for help to take care of the meat. We prepared to dry or jerk some of it. We drove four forked sticks in the ground, about ten feet apart in a square. Across these we laid poles, and then smaller sticks on which to lay the meat, after it was cut in thin slices. Under this scaffold we built a fire to keep the flies away and to assist the sun in drying the meat. We were several days thus occupied, and during this time I went with the Indians down the Wallowa Valley, a most beautiful one, lying along the south side of Wallowa Lake. On the north of the lake the mountains rose several thousand feet, rather abruptly. Joseph's village was an ideal one; it occupied the site on which now stands Enterprise City.

While the Indians were taking care of the elk killed, Chief Joseph was several times at our camp. On one of these occasions he related the following incident in the history of his people:

"A long time ago," he said, "I don't know how

long, but think it was as long as two men can live (meaning 200 years), our tribe was very strong, and we had many warriors, and went every summer out into the buffalo country to hunt. Once our people met a band of Blackfeet warriors and had a great battle. There were a great many Blackfeet, and we had only a few warriors. Red Wolf was the chief, and he lost nearly all his braves. There was great sorrow in the village when he returned almost alone and told what the Blackfeet had done.

"All that winter our people made bows and arrows, and when the spring came, Red Wolf gathered all his warriors and went to fight the Blackfeet. They did not go to the Blackfeet country, for that is a long way off, but found a large band of them in the buffalo country, and had a great battle. Nearly all the Blackfeet were killed, and Red Wolf got 2000 horses and many scalps, and none of his warriors were killed. When he came back home our people were glad, and danced many days.

"Every year Red Wolf went to the buffalo country and fought the Blackfeet; sometimes we lost many warriors. Red Wolf got old and died, but still our people fought every summer, and took many scalps. Young Red Wolf, the old chief's son, led the warriors, and we were a great people. Every boy went to the buffalo country as soon as he was big enough to fight.

Once, when Young Red Wolf and a great many braves were out hunting buffalo, the Blackfeet came on them while they were all asleep and killed a great many and followed the rest. Every day they fought, but the Blackfeet were so many, as many as the blades of grass on the hills. When Red Wolf crossed the lake he had only a few braves and he could fight no more. The Blackfeet camped on the other side of the lake, and built great fires and shouted and danced; but no fires were in our village, and the women wailed for our lost braves.

"Red Wolf had one child, a daughter, Wahluna. She was very sorry for her people and loved her father, who could fight no more, but said they would all be killed when the Blackfeet came around the lake. At night, while they were all wailing for the dead, Wahluna went down in the willows by the lake, and when everyone had gone away from the water, she got in her canoe and paddled across the lake to the camp of the Blackfeet. Her paddle made no sound, and they did not hear her until she stood by the fire and said: 'I am Wahluna, Red Chief's child. I want to talk to the great chief of your people.'

"Then the great chief said: 'What words has the daughter of Red Wolf to speak? My ears are open.'

"Wahluna said: 'Our warriors are nearly all gone, only a few are left, and our women and children are wailing for our dead. It is dark in our village, and we have no fires, for we are afraid of the great chief of the Blackfeet. Red Wolf says tomorrow all will die. When you come you will only find old men and women and children; you can kill the old people and take the young girls and children for slaves; but when you come to your own village your women and young girls cannot hear your warriors shout, for we will wail loud for our dead braves, and your women will wail with us, and there will be no joy in your village. You have many scalps of our young warriors, and do not want the scalps of old men and women. If you go to your own country and do not come to our village, then our fires can burn again. We can never fight the great chief again, for our braves are all dead.'

"Then Wahluna laid her face in the sand, and did not move. Then Tlesca, a young chief, the son of the great chief, laid his robe upon her shoulders and said: 'My heart is sore with yours, and I will not kill any more of your people.'

"Then the great chief was angry and said: 'Her people are dogs. Let the brave Chief Tlesca take his robe from her shoulders that she may die.'

"But Tlesca said: 'The daughter of Red Wolf, who has fought our bravest warriors along the trail for a thousand miles, is not a dog. For one whole moon he has fought our braves by day and by night. He had nothing to eat, and his knees were weak; we could see him stagger when he ran; but when he turned to fight for his people, his heart was great. I am the only one of all our warriors who would fight him alone; my shoulder is broken by his war club. My robe is on the maiden's shoulders; I will not take it away. I have spoken.'

"Tlesca was a great warrior, and the Great Chief loved him and said: 'The great warrior Tlesca has spoken and his words are good. I will lay my robe on his.' Then Wahluna knew her people might live, and went back to her canoe.

"When she took her paddle, Tlesca was standing there, and said: 'When twelve moons are passed Wahluna will listen in the middle of the night and she will hear a great owl down by the lake. Come when you hear the owl and I will speak.'

"And Wahluna counted the moons, and when twelve were passed, she listened, when all in the village were asleep, and she heard the great owl down by the lake. Then she put her robe on and went through the village. Her feet made no sound, and no one saw her. At the edge of the lake she found Tlesca. He said: 'The maidens of the Blackfeet are fair, and many look on Tlesca, for he is a great warrior; but his heart is with Wahluna, and he wants her for his wife.'

"Wahluna said: 'My people would kill you, for their hearts are sore, for the wolves have gnawed the bones of their young men.'

"Tlesca said: 'When six moons have passed, Wahluna will listen in the middle of the night, when all are asleep, and she will hear a grey wolf across the lake. Let Wahluna come, and Tlesca will speak.'

"Wahluna counted the moons, and when six were gone and all were asleep in the middle of the night, she heard the grey wolf across the lake. Then she took her canoe and went across the lake and found Tlesca. He said: 'When the sun is over the great mountain I will come to the Red Wolf's village with my father, the Great Chief of the Blackfeet, and all our chiefs and many great warriors, and we will smoke the peace pipe together, and the Blackfeet and Red Wolf's people will be brothers, and Red Wolf can come to hunt the buffalo, and we will catch fish from your lake.'

"Wahluna went back to the village and told her father that when the sun was over the great mountain the Great Chief and his warriors would come and smoke the pipe of peace with the Wallowas. When the Blackfeet came, they smoked together and were brothers. The Great Chief said: 'Tlesca is a great warrior, and his heart is with Wahluna, and he wants her for his wife.'

"Red Wolf sent runners to all his friends, the Nez Perces, the Kiyouses, and the Yakimas, and they came, and there was a great wedding, and Wahluna said she would sit in Tlesca's lodge. The young men bought deer, bear, and elk from the mountains, and the girls caught fish in the lakes, and they had a great feast, and all were very happy.

"Tlesca and Wahluna got into a canoe, when the sun went down, and went out on the lake, for it was very fair to look at. All the people stood on the shore and watched their canoe. Then they saw a great serpent come out of the water, and the canoe was turned over, and Tlesca and Wahluna were never seen again.

"Then the Blackfeet went back to their country and said the Great Spirit was angry because they had made peace with Red Wolf and his people."

After a few moments, I asked the young chief if the story was a true one, or just a story told to please the children.

"O," he said, "it is all true; I have heard my people tell it many times, and have heard some of the Blackfeet warriors tell it, too."

"But," I asked, "do you believe that a great snake came and swallowed Tlesca and Wahluna?"

"No," he answered, "one big wind, one big wave; that's all."

A fisherman from Walla Walla, now dead, told Mrs. Wiggins that the monster, as long as a rowboat, surfaced right near his boat. "He probably got the best look at it," she said.

Mrs. Wiggins believes that the monster is still in the lake. "I'll swear there's a big one in there," she said. "You can see it when the lake's quiet and the light's right."

According to a story published in **The Oregonian** in 1950, Mr. and Mrs. H. C. Wicklander, of Joseph, and Joe Tatone, of Portland, saw two creatures, one "about 16 feet long," and the other about eight feet long, feeding on bluebacks at the head of the Lake. "Sideways it (the largest of the pair) presented the outline of a great trout or perhaps a shark, but rather blunt-nosed and with no dorsal fin visible. The head-on view of the thing gave the impression of a wide buffalo head, perhaps two feet across with eyes about 14 inches apart."

In the same article, Mr. and Mrs. Bob Reese, residents of Wallowa County, reported having seen a similar "monster fish" in 1932, from their boat, about 300 feet from the west shore. "Near what seemed the bottom they saw a great fish as long or longer than

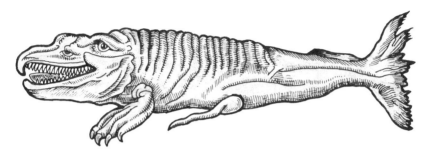

their 11-foot boat. They crossed and recrossed the monster, which seemed not to be bothered by them."

Wallowa Lake is home to other legends, too. When we were children we were told that the lake is bottomless, and that it is connected to the Great Lakes by a subterranean river. An article published in 1951 in the **Wallowa County Chieftain** stated, "The lake yields up none of its drowning victims, who presumably are carried away by this strange creature who lurks hundreds of feet below the surface." My sisters told me of a fisherman who drowned in Wallowa Lake. His body washed up on the shore of Lake Erie.

The Laughing Devil
in
Laughing Devil Canyon

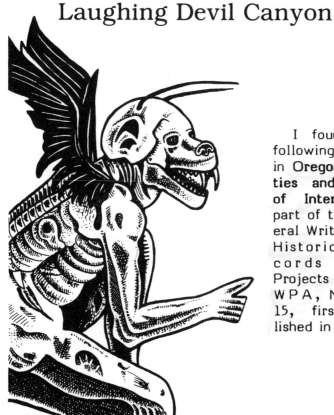

I found the following story in **Oregon Oddities and Items of Interest,** a part of the Federal Writers and Historical Records Survey Projects of the WPA, Number 15, first published in 1938.

Back in the 1850's, during the various gold rushes that swept through the west, two prospectors decided to search for gold in the wilds of the Curry County hills. They bought their supplies at a general store, where the storekeeper warned them that nobody entered or remained in Laughing Devil Canyon after dark. Nevertheless, the two miners headed across country to the mouth of the canyon.

They reached their destination about noon and without hesitation started up between the canyon's gloomy walls. All afternoon they worked their way slowly up the gulch, prospecting as they went. Toward sunset they found gold and named their claim the Pick and Shovel Mine.

As night settled down, the two prospectors sat by their campfire planning how they would spend their new-found wealth. Suddenly horrible laughter echoed along the canyon walls. Closer and closer the laughter sounded, so terrifying that even the thought of gold could keep them there no longer. They fled and another lost mine was added to Oregon's mining legends.

The
Steens Mountain Ghost

The first time I went to Steens Mountain was back in 1954. My mother and father packed my sisters and I and our Navy surplus canvas tent--with tent poles bigger than your arm--into the 1947 Buick that had belonged to my grandfather, and we headed south for a couple of glorious camping weeks. Our destination was Fish Lake, about 14 miles uphill from Frenchglen, the hamlet at the base of the mountain. In those 14 miles, my father told us, we would climb 1400 feet up the mountain. What he didn't know was that we would have three flat tires on that same stretch of rough road.

Fish Lake and a 160 acres surrounding it were owned by Harry and Florabelle Smith, a kind, if profane, couple who spent much of each summer in an A-frame cabin they had constructed on the lakeshore.

The only other building was the outhouse, built on the hillside a hundred or so feet from the lake.

Florabelle was a large woman with a reddish face, silver hair, and a vocabulary powerful enough to stop a muleskinner dead in his tracks. "Oh, shiiii...," she would begin, looking about to see if my sisters or I were within hearing distance. If we were, her epithet was quickly watered down to "Oh, shiiii-miny!" Harry Smith was as thin as Florabelle was fleshy, as subdued as she was explosive. He told me the best places to fish from the bank, to watch out for the hawks that nested in the aspen trees across the lake, and promised me that one of these days, if I was out there by the lake just as evening stole a-cross the mountain, I'd see Old Rocky, the legendary lunker trout who lived in the depths of the lake. Old Rocky had been hooked many times, but never caught. Harry had seen him often enough, and even hooked him a couple of times, but always the wily trout had escaped. He looked, Harry said, "Like a fence post," when he broke the surface, and he could jump clear over a fishing boat. Harry had seen him do it. If I were lucky, he might even take my fly.

Fish Lake in those days was a kid's dream. We were there in July, and still the snow lingered in the shady spots on the far bank. The lake was small, a clear alpine jewel in the sagebrush far from civiliz-ation, fringed by aspen trees, home to fierce hawks that dived on fishermen who ventured too near their nests. "Quaking aspen," my mother called these gaunt trees, and they did quake, two-toned leaves rattling the breeze and shimmering in the thin sunlight.

Best of all, though, Fish Lake was the end of the road. It was a mighty rough road, and not many people thought enough of their solitude in those days to take the trouble to follow it. The only people up there, in all that vast and magnificent stillness, were the Smiths, a couple of Basque sheepherders, and my family.

It was a wonderful time for us all. With my .22 rifle and my old dog Fritz, I wandered through the sagebrush around the lake for hours. "Don't shoot toward the lake," my father warned. "Look out for rattlesnakes," said my mother. I never saw a rattlesnake, but Fritz and I saw antelope with big, soft eyes. We surprised them and saw them vanish like phantoms in the sagebrush. We saw coyotes, loping easily, devouring distance, and we heard them laughing like demons at some hellish roast in the night. We saw hawks, majestic gliders riding the thermals, eyes fixed on the floor. They would hover, plummet, rise with a snake or rabbit clutched in their talons and soar off to dine in less crowded surroundings. A boy could be a real explorer for hours every day in a place like that.

We visited the Basques in their camp, and my sister Tricia fell in love for the first time, with a shepherd called Tony. That she was only ten and he probably twice that didn't matter to her, but it mattered to my father, who seemed to see Tricia a little differently after that. Tony returned Tricia's love in the form of bread, huge round loaves that he baked using hot rocks in a hole-in-the-ground oven and brought to our camp almost daily after our visit to his camp.

There was only one boat at the lake, and no motor. I was just old enough that my parents let me take the boat out by myself. My sisters weren't old enough to go with me, so I rowed to the middle of the lake by myself, smug in the knowledge that their eyes were locked jealously on every stroke of the oars. I took my pole and drifted with the breeze. I worked hard to perfect my cast, and soon I could put a fly down softly on the lake's surface thirty or forty feet from the boat, even casting into the breeze. Soon, very soon, I felt, I'd be good enough to fool Old Rocky.

When I wasn't using the boat, my father, ever the bait and lure fisherman, rowed my mother round and round the lake, trolling with spinners and worms. Fish Lake was the only place in the world, I think, where I could catch more fish than he did. I caught them on flies from the boat when he was on shore, and, when he and my mother were trolling, I caught them on flies from the rickety old dock. Nobody ever caught Old Rocky.

But all this is a digression. You want to know about the ghost. Okay, but bear with me just a little farther.

Fish Lake is a state park now, and last time I was there it was surrounded by motor homes with California license plates. The A-frame cabin is gone, and the outhouse was replaced by an official set of bad-smelling, green Oregon State toilets. There were boats all over lake and dozens of campers lounged about the shore in aluminum-and-plastic chairs, listening to portable radios and drinking Coors beer.

The ghost. There is a ghost, some say, on Steens Mountain, but no one ever sees it. It is recognizable only by the sound it makes, that of a motor running, and it can only be heard on land owned by the Alvord and Mann Lake Ranches.

The Ghost
of
Enchanted Prairie

Enchanted Prairie, writes Lewis MacArthur, in **Oregon Geographic Names,** is "an open spot alongside the Coos Bay-Roseburg Highway approximately four miles east of Bridge and about 25 miles east of Myrtle Point. In the summer of 1943 Mrs. Alice B. Maloney of Berkeley, California, wrote the compiler that the place had a special significance for the Indians, who buried their dead there in a sort of cavern. Enchanted Prairie Post Office was established January 9, 1871...The name of the post office was changed to Angora August 3, 1883." Angora Post Office closed less than a year later.

I found this story in **Oregon Native Son,** Volume 1, Number 5, published in September, 1899.

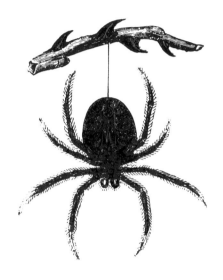

In 1855 there was a general Indian war in Oregon and Washington territories. There was a confederation of nearly all of the tribes in those regions for the purpose of banishing or exterminating the "Boston Men", as they called the white settlers.

Hostilities were commenced without warning, and some of the outlying and isolated settlements were almost annihilated. The theater of the conflict extended from southern Oregon to northern Washington; no part of this great area being entirely exempt except the Willamette Valley, which was too populous to be attacked, until the other sections should be overcome, and portions of the northern coast regions, where the Indians were too sluggish to be aroused. Intelligence of the outbreak spread rapidly, and very soon a call to arms was made in all of the settlements, and nearly every man capable for service volunteered for the war.

103

The conflict was exceptionally severe in southern Oregon. The conditions there were inviting for a successful incursion. The physical features are favorable for such a warfare. It is a country of mountains and valleys, and in those days the settlements were separated and sparse. The Indians who roamed over that region were a vigorous, bold and warlike people, and resented the occupancy of their hunting grounds by an alien race.

Prior to this, there had been spasmodic uprisings by different bands into which the tribes were divided, but, because of lack of unity, they had been easily overcome. Now, however, by combining the bands and tribes for concert of action, the savages hoped to rid the country of the hated intruders. Around their council fires, in the almost inaccessible mountains, they had matured their plans, and the secret of them was well guarded.

The attack was made before their purpose was suspected. The Rogue River country received the first blow. The Rogue River Indians were assisted in this onslaught, in addition to others, by the Umpquas and the south coast tribes, probably in consideration of like assistance to be given them in prosecuting the war in their territories. The Umpqua Valley is separated from the Rogue River country by the Cow Creek Mountains, and both of these from the coast by the Coast Range of mountains.

Hostilities had not reached the coast, or Umpqua, at the time the event about to be related occurred. However, experience had taught those early settlers to be prepared for trouble with the Indians on short notice. Places of rendezvous and defense were in readiness to which they could flee in time of danger. These places were usually centrally located and easily accessible. With such precautions, if only short warning were given, the larger part, if not all, of the settlers might reach these places of safety.

By some means, intelligence of the outbreak on Rogue River quickly reached the Coos Bay settlement. This settlement, as its name indicates, was on the coast. With this news came the information that a band of warriors was on the way to the coast, and also a rumor that a larger band purposed to cross the Cow Creek Mountains and lay waste the settlements in Umpqua Valley.

Being warned of their danger, the settlers around Coos Bay gathered at their place of refuge and prepared for defense; but in their distress they did not forget their countrymen in Umpqua. Perhaps they had not been warned of the impending danger. What was their duty in the matter? A consultation was held, and all agreed that a message of warning ought to be sent. Who would undertake to convey it was the next proposition. Immediately Enoch Anderson arose and expressed a willingness to go.

He was a young man of striking personality. His physique denoted great power of endurance. He was tall, sinewy, lithe and agile. He was not a stranger to any of those present. They all knew the message could not be entrusted to better hands. His courage had often been tested and never found wanting. When danger called he always answered. Endowed with an iron will and a vigorous intellect, difficulties were but playthings in his pathway. Although not trained in the curriculum of the schools, his mind was so strengthened and broadened by observation, reflection and reading, that he believed that superstition had no lurking place in it. His world was free from invasion by ghosts, apparitions, and all other supernatural agencies.

The proposed journey, however, would be the supreme test of courage. The distance to be traveled was about 60 miles by the shortest route. The way was over rugged mountains and through dense forests, infested by savage beasts and possibly by more savage men. Only at wide intervals were there openings in the great woods. The journey would be exceedingly lonely, and, under the circumstances, very trying for the nerves.

The best horse in the settlement was furnished him, food for his use on the way was provided, and he was well equipped for the journey. There were two trails leading from Coos Bay to the Umpqua. One of them following, as nearly as possible, the summits of ridges and spurs, was less rugged but considerably longer than the other, which instead of following crossed over them wherever feasible. He chose the more direct route.

When his choice became known, many of his friends endeavored to dissuade him from it. This trail passed through "Enchanted Prairie", which, if he started at the appointed time, he would reach about midnight. This prairie, according to legend, was haunted by innumerable ghosts. It was believed by the Indians to be the nightly rendezvous of the unhappy spirits of the dead; that it was the wailing place of the "cultus" (from the Chinook jargon, meaning "of little worth") shades, whose misery was only equaled by their hatred of incarnate forms; that in the night time they came to that secluded and charming spot because it was the nearest approach to the happy hunting grounds they could hope to attain. At such times they resented any intrusion from the living, and no Indian would approach it between the hours of sunset and sunrise.

Some of the whites were convinced that the belief of the Indians was well founded, for when by chance they had come near it on moonlight nights, strange apparitions had appeared, undefinable forms had flitted before them and mocking voices had answered their calls. Although men of unchallenged courage, they confessed a fear of tempting the shadowy host and would not attempt to enter it after nightfall.

Enoch Anderson's mind was too well fortified to be disturbed with such phantoms. To all of their entreaties he made plain that it was his opinion that the spirit of an Indian clothed with flesh and blood was more to be dreaded than their ghostly shadows from the nether world. He smiled at their credulity and adhered to his decision. As soon as the preparations were completed he mounted the horse,

106

good-byes were exchanged and he rode away.

It was about the middle of the afternoon when he left the settlement and entered the forest; and such a forest only those who have visited the timbered regions of the Pacific coast can imagine. It was early summer, and not a cloud flecked the infinite blue, but so thickly stood the gigantic trees that barely a gleam of sunlight reached the ground. Such forests are grand, but the darkness of them soon becomes depressing. Self-poised and bouyant as Enoch was, the silence and shadows which surrounded him and the somber pictures of what might occur before his message could be delivered, which would now and again, unbidden, image themselves on his mind, repressed his judgment and quickened his imagination.

Bye and bye the sun went down and the gloom thickened. Although the full moon coursed her way among the stars, his path amid the trees was profoundly dark, but rapidly and without halt he rode on. He gave rein to his horse, and it instinctively kept the track. Over rugged hill and tangled vale he kept his pauseless way.

About midnight he reached the summit of a high ridge, and through an opening in the woods he beheld in a valley before him the famous "Enchanted Prairie" reposing in the moonlight. It was a scene of rare beauty. To our hero who had been for many hours depressed by the gloom and darkness, it appeared like a radiant gem set in the encircling mountains. He paused a moment to enjoy the vision.

The legend which had given this lovely and picturesque spot such an uncanny reputation came to mind, but was instantly dismissed as a foul defamation of a most beautiful and peaceful locality, for not anywhere was there the slightest indication that this charming bit of landscape was an annex of pandemonium. With a light heart he again went forward down the mountain path. As he drew near to this place of light and beauty his spirit revived and all dejection passed away. Cheerful thoughts and purposes for the immediate future dissipated distrust and forebodings. What a relief to have a respite from the dreary shadows! There he would pause for a little rest and refreshment. While reposing his faithful animal might feed on the luxuriant grass which grew in the vale.

The base of the mountain was nearly reached. The delightful resting place was just ahead. All seemed well. The profound quietude was unbroken save by the soft sighing of a gentle wind as it passed through the treetops. No shadow of apprehension was on Enoch's mind, but owing to the strain on his nerves during his long and lonely ride through the wilderness, he was more susceptible to abnormal impressions than he was conscious of. As he was emerging from the heavy woods into the scattering timber that fringed the prairie, his horse suddenly stopped and stood as if transfixed with terror. He was convulsed with a tremor of fright. Coaxing and urging would not induce him to advance.

Enoch was perplexed. He had not noticed the slightest cause for such alarm. No voice or startling sound had disturbed the stillness of the night. He looked carefully on either side, but nothing which might excite the fear of either man or beast could be seen.

He then removed a bough in front of him and peered forward into the entrance of the prairie, and there but a few paces before him an object met his vision which could but appall the stoutest heart. Its aspect was human, but still not human. He had never beheld its like before. Its form was attenuated but of prodigious height. It was arrayed in a gauze-like robe of glistening white. Its face seemed slightly averted, but he caught for an instant the gleam of its awful eyes and they seemed to challenge him with super-human fierceness.

Enoch was startled. He gazed a moment in a dazed way, and then the dreadful thought flashed upon his mind that this unearthly form was a ghostly sentinel guarding the bivouac of the dead and lost. Ah! the scouted legend was no shadow after all. He

108

experienced a feeling more akin to fear than he had ever known. He looked upon it some moments longer in profound silence, but the feared presence heeded him not, and with calm dignity marched back and forth, to and fro, across his pathway.

A great awe came over Enoch as in the silence and loneliness of the great wilderness the conviction grew that he was indeed confronted by a spirit from the nether world. The longer he gazed the stronger this conviction became. A tremor smote him and a clammy perspiration moistened his brow. An impulse to turn and run seized him, but his pride and will even in this dire extremity, had not deserted him, and they restrained him. To retreat without an effort to advance would be shameful.

Summoning all the force of his great will, he rallied sufficient courage to address the weird sentinel. In a loud voice he asked: "Who are you and what is your mission here?"

The silent sentinel heeded not, but continued its noiseless march back and forth, to and fro, across the pathway, but from all around the vale and from many voices came the mocking response: "Who are you and what is your mission here?" The result was not quieting to agitated nerves. That this terrible form which confronted him was not a creature of the imagination was evident. Had not his horse, which heeded no legend, and was endowed with no imagination, seen it first? Then the regular, rhythmic way in which it marched back and forth, to and fro, across the entrance to the forbidden spot was too real for a phantom.

All efforts at disillusion could not banish it. No, he could not be mistaken. It was a veritable form, and no shadow, or, if a shade, it was tangible and prepared to withstand flesh and blood. Logic might deride and philosophy scorn, but the evidence of vision could not be set aside. And those mocking, answering voices, were they not emanations from spirits which haunted the vale? The legend was no myth, and at any moment the pale horde might pour forth

109

to wreak vengeance on the intruder.

Such were the thoughts which surged through Enoch's brain. The stress was great. His courage was tested as it never had been. In all the variety experience of a wild, pioneer life, amid scenes of turbulence and strife, in no situation had his courage forsaken him or his eyes beheld the object his heart feared.

This was a peculiar condition. Here at the hour of midnight, in the solitude of the mountain vale, remote from any of human kind, confronted by disquieted and perhaps malignant spirits, what would the outcome be?

The question of what he should do pressed hard. Should he retrace his steps and take the other road or risk all and go forward? To go back meant a delay of almost two days. The terrible possibilities involved in such delay arose vividly before him. The hideous war cry of the savage, mingled with the terrified and despairing scream of helpless women and innocent children, seemed to ring in his ears. Such a dastardly thought must not be entertained. He must not be false to his trust. He would try again.

He raised his voice once more and shouted: "O stranger, from regions unknown, why do you haunt this lonely vale?"

"Why do you haunt this lonely vale?" came in a confused and mocking murmur from the prairie beyond, but the undaunted and undisturbed figure, with "stately step and slow," marched back and forth, to and fro, across the pathway.

At the last call Enoch thought he detected a slight tremor of the attenuated form and a faint but malignant smile flit over its cadaverous features. Each moment the situation became more trying. The strain of a great perplexity was almost distracting the young man. Notwithstanding all this, he retained a measure of self-possession.

For a little while he was undecided. The path seemed most effectually blocked with a foe with which he was powerless to cope. The impulse to turn and retrace his steps was almost overpowering, but he was restrained by the thought of the humiliation to which he would be subjected when he met his associates at the fort, and was asked to explain the cause of his retreat. What could he say? How could he explain? He knew that a foe of more than mortal prowess hedged the way, but how could he convince them that he knew? What evidence had he to present? He grasped the dilemma even under the shadow of the ghostly presence. The taunt would be that he, whose name was a synonym for bravery throughout that region, had been frightened by a voiceless and unaggressive figure, abandoned a mission of the supremest importance, and fled from he knew not what.

And what would that one think whose trustful and admiring eyes beheld in him the personification of manliness, courage and chivalry, when she learned that he had been frightened by a ghost, and had abandoned to an awful fate her sisters in Umpqua? This thought moved him as none other had. It led to a quick decision. He would go through then and on that trail or die. It would be preferable to perish alone, unnoted, and let his unsepulchered bones bleach in this solitary place, than to return with the odor of cowardice upon him and endure the scorn of his foes, the jeers of his rivals and the pity of his friends.

With this resolution came the courage of despair, and bracing himself in the saddle he applied whip and spur to his terrified animal and when it at last dashed forward, Enoch exclaimed with the utmost power of his voice: "Thou ghastly form that blocks my way, be you fiend or be you devil, avaunt, for my mission brooks no delay!"

But the awful presence, with grim indifference, kept its measured and steady pace back and forth, to and fro, across the pathway. But onward rushed horse and rider, the young man with curdling blood and heart almost paralyzed, but with a determination as sublime as ever animated a hero.

The dreadful form is almost reached. With a

quickened movement it turned toward Enoch as if preparing to receive its prey. Its eyes gleamed like points of light and glared on him with prodigious wrath and unquailing courage. The next moment he grappled it, its long arms stretched out and enfolded him, a cold gauzelike film enmeshed his hands and face, a thrill of horror passed through him, but almost immediately he rallied, and, viewing himself from head to feet, exclaimed in a suppressed but intense manner, "A spider web, by Jupiter!"

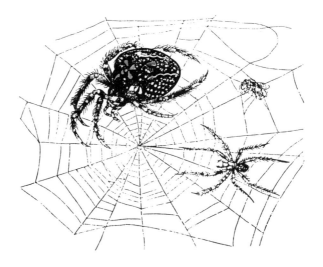

And so it was. Pendant from a gouth of stately oak was a spider web. It reached from the limb almost to the ground, its gossamer like threads were wet with the dews of the night, and as seen in the moonlight appeared like a veritable garment for ghostly equipment. The gentle wind swayed it back and forth across the path and imagination did the rest.

GEORGE STOWELT

112

The Haunted
McAlder Homestead

Old Man McAlder homesteaded in the hills outside of Roseburg before there was a Roseburg. He
married an Indian woman, the daughter of a medicine
man, who had inherited some of her father's knowledge of magic, and they lived together on their
homestead for many years. They were a kind and
generous couple who loved each other deeply.

One day Mrs. McAlder got sick. The sickness
lingered and, after a week or so, she told her husband that she was about to die. She looked into his
eyes and told him that she had been very happy with
him and with their life together in the cabin they
had built on the homestead. Then she looked around
the cabin and said "My spirit will always be in this
house. Any time a person is lost and comes upon this
cabin there will be a fire going, sweet water in the
well, and bread in the oven." Then she died.

Old Man McAlder didn't want to stay on the
homestead alone, so he moved into Roseburg and a
year or so later he, too, died.

Years later a party of surveyors were working
on the land near the McAlder homestead. They became separated and one man was lost. He walked and
walked. Night came, it started to rain, and still he
was stumbling through the brush. Suddenly, he saw a
light on the hillside through the rain, and he walked
toward it.

The surveyor found a small cabin in a clearing.
Inside, a fire burned in the fireplace, bread baked in
the oven, and drinking water, already drawn from the
well, waited in a pitcher on the table, but no one
was around. He dried himself by the fire, ate the
bread, drank the water, and fell into the clean, dry

bed, where he slept soundly until morning.

The next day he rejoined the other surveyors. When he told them the story of the deserted cabin, no one believed him, so he insisted on showing them. They all trooped up through the woods to the old McAlder homestead, but when they got there all they found was a shell of a cabin with the roof half fallen in.

The cabin is still there, up above Cougar Creek, and it's in worse shape now than it was when that dubious party of surveyors looked at it years ago. But if you were lost, some say, the old McAlder homestead would be a very nice place to stay.

The Galesville Hotel

The Galesville Hotel is gone, but you can still hear the northbound stage when it stops there at 11:00 each morning as it did regularly in the early days of Douglas County. Stagecoach doors slam and people talk and move about--but you won't see them.

This story first appeared in the **Roseburg News-Review** in February, 1973. It was given to me by the author, Lavola J. Bakken, a research specialist at the Douglas County Museum in Roseburg.

Pioneer spirits haunt
Galesville hotel site

by Lavola J. Bakken

Omar and Simon heard the car door slam and the children laugh and squeal at the same time Peggy heard it. They exchanged Siamese cat-eyed stares, jumped from their napping place on the sunny kitchen

HOTEL PROPERTY OF D.A.LEVENS, GALESVILLE, DOUGLAS CO.

This drawing of the Galesville Hotel appeared in Walling's History of Southern Oregon, published in 1884.

window sill, and hid in the stairwell. Omar and Simon don't like noisy youngsters. Peggy Van Vlake dried her hands at the sink and went out to welcome her grand-children, she thought. When she opened the back door, there was no one there.

115

A long lane leads to Peggy and Charlie Van Vlake's home from the Azalea road and the house sits about an equal distance from Interstate 5, across Cow Creek in southern Douglas County.

"A car couldn't come in our yard, turn around and disappear that quickly," Peggy explained. "Charlie said I just imagined the whole thing the first time this happened, but since then he hasn't been so sure, especially as the cats hear it, too."

Peggy looks directly at you with friendly hazel eyes and pushes auburn hair back from her tanned face while she talks. You believe her. There's something matter-of-fact about her speeh when she tells you about the ghosts, like any other housewife would repeat a recipe for sweet pickles.

Strange things happen here in her farm house, but there's no feeling of menace. Family and friends wander in and out as she talks. The coffee pot is on. When someone leaves, Peggy calls out, "You all come back!"

Charlie Van Vlake smiles and doesn't say much when you ask him if he believes that ghosts haunt his house. He'd rather talk about his fat white Charolais cattle that graze the Cow Creek bank. Or how this farm was once a stagecoach stop called Galesville when Colonel Stone ran six-horse coaches through the Sexton and Siskiyou Mountains.

Here, in 1882, Dan Levens built a hotel and a livery barn that sheltered upwards of 90 horses. The northbound stage stopped regularly at 11 in the morning, the same hour Peggy often hears the coach rattle up and let out ghostly passengers.

Charlie admits to seeing some things, like the bottle that jumped out of the waste basket, but for explanation he still gives you just a smile.

"Van, Kelly, Darren and my daughter were all here," Peggy said. "We finished drinking some wine and she put the bottle in that waste basket sitting right there in the corner. Pretty soon, it jumped out and rolled across the floor. You know, that's kind of

116

hard for a square bottle to do.

"The first time I noticed anything was when I came up here in '66. My daughter from Georgia came out and we were getting ready to paint the living room. We were taking the venetian blinds down, and all at once we heard two women talking. Both of us heard it, but we couldn't tell what they were saying. 'Charlotte,' I says, 'someone's here.'

"It was August and the doors were open. I looked out and she looked out the other end of the room, but neither of us saw a soul. Just two women talking like they were visiting, but there wasn't a body on the place 'sides us."

The Van Vlakes' comfortable living room with its wide hearth doesn't look like a Gothic ghost castle any more than Peggy's generous-sized kitchen looks haunted.

"Then we had trouble with a stairway window that wouldn't stay locked," Peggy continued. "The boys or me'd lock that window at night on the way to bed and in the morning it'd be plum open. Finally I had Darren jam the lock to keep it shut." Peggy indicated a small window on the stair landing, about halfway up.

"Los of times I'm sitting down here and hear things going on up those stairs. Hasn't been over two-three weeks ago we were all sitting here and I says, 'Van, what's upstairs?' and he says, 'I'm not going to go see!' Sounded like somebody leafing through magazines or turning pages in books. It wasn't the cats, because they were laying on top of the television. Finally I went up there, but—nothing."

Another person who recalls the mysterious atmosphere of the place is Cecile Ramondo of Sebastopol, California.

"I remember the old hotel or stage depot, the one that burned here in 1931. It was monstrous and spooky," she said. "I spent part of each summer there from the time I was a little girl until I married. My uncle, Clifford Smith, ran the place as the Azalea

117

River Ranch."

At that time, a huge porch encircled the inn on three sides and the door to the upstairs was at the rear of the building with no entrance from the inside. This caused much speculation because originally there could have been inside access through a door at the end of a small hall which then opened on a blank wall.

"There were covered peepholes, too, although who 'peeped' at whom, we never knew," Cecile said. "About the haunts, what can I say? Kids are always making up tales and the place certainly had an air of mystery about it. The inn sat in an isolated area at that time, and the summer lightning that crackled on the clouded Canyon Mountains added to the eerie atmosphere of the whole ranch.

"I never really felt afraid here except when my older cousins set out deliberately to frighten me. Once one of the boys locked me in an upstairs room and because of the density of the walls and floors, no one heard my screams and yells until I was missed at dinner. Quite some time passed before I ventured up those stairs again."

Clifford Smith built the present house to replace the old inn after it burned. This is Charlie Van Vlake's house now and it rests on the foundation of the old hotel. Five fire-scarred maples, planted by Dan Levens 90 years ago, shade Charlie's porches. Earlier, a log stockade sheltered besieged settlers here during the Southern Oregon Indian Wars.

To fight that war, on October 10, 1855, Captain Rinearson enrolled 35 men at Cow Creek following massacres the previous day by the Rogue Indians. The captain stationed his men to guard the miles of wilderness road between Jacksonville and Roseburg. These volunteers manned forts at the Canyon, Levens Station, Turners, and farther south at Harness and Two Good's Grave Creek House.

Following the fortification, the Indians vanished from the settlements for two weeks. They gathered in the mountains and conspired at war councils to rid their valleys of the settlers and the miners.

On October 24, the warriors returned and attacked some hog drovers from Lane County. H. Bailey was killed instantly, his brother and three others wounded. On that same day, Indians burned houses and barns of Turner, Bray, Fortune, Redfield and one other neighbor of Daniel Levens.

Redfield's farm adjoined Levens on the south. Redfield hurried his family into the wagon and whipped the team towards the Smith stockade. First the Rogues wounded Mrs. Redfield, then they killed the horses. Redfield carried his wife on his back to safety in Smith's fort. The Indian bullet that lodged in her knee gave her a limp for the rest of her life.

Writing of the events that happened next, William L. Byars, pioneer mail carrier between Oakland and Yreka from 1856 to 1858, said: "The settlers and travelers on the road assembled at the Smith place, the Dan Levens place and the Hardy Ellif place, all three being protected by stockades. The Indians burned all the other houses in the valley. They attacked the Smith place and the battle lasted for several hours, but no one was killed.

"When no Indians appeared at the Levens place, Johnson and Mynatt volunteered to go to the top of a high hill near by and reconnoitre. Before they reached the summit, the Indians opened fire on them and shot Mynatt through the lungs He ran partially down the hill and fell. Johnson helped him up and tried to assist him. The Indians were shooting all the time.

"John Fortune, seeing the trouble from the fort, jumped on a horse and hurried to their assistance. He got there and Johnson put Mynatt on the horse before Fortune, who put his horse to a full run, carried Mynatt to safety. But Johnson had no more than placed Mynatt on the horse when a bullet struck him and he fell dead. The Indians, there in sight of all the garrison, scalped and desecrated Johnson's body with much screeching and tantalizing epithets. They didn't come within gunshot of the fort...

119

"Then the savages all went down the creek (where Glendale is now) and made camp, boasted and feasted for several days before doing other bloody work."

Some people say a place must be marked by some horrible event before ghosts take up residence. What could strike more terror to a helpless, outnumbered cadre of volunteers than to see a companion killed and scalped?

Peggy Van Vlake didn't know about Johnson's death when she first heard the stagecoach. Now, when the 11 a.m. stage stops and leaves its invisible, noisy passengers, she wonders if they are stopping for a leisurely lunch or if they are fleeing for their lives from the Rogue River Indians.

Some neighbors say Peggy imagines these things, but Simon and Omar know. The cats run and hide from real children because they don't like to be mauled, and they also run for the stairwell when that morning stagecoach rolls in.

The Hunchback
of
Lithia Park

In the 1920's there lived in Ashland a hunchbacked boy, the son of a woodcutter, who contracted a disease which caused hair to grow all over his body. This boy, who became known as the Dog-faced Boy of Ashland, supported himself by selling pencils and stealing from cars and wagons. He was often seen with a gunny sack over his shoulder going through the wagons and cars of people attending the chataqua which would set up in the area where the

Oregon Shakespearean Theatre is today. One day, about 1926, the dog-faced boy disappeared. There was speculation that he had been murdered, but no body was ever found, and no one was charged with the crime.

In the 1960's the dog-faced boy appeared again, near the theatre, and, with the gunny sack over his shoulder, resumed his career of stealing from parked cars. The police were called several times, but each time, as they arrived, the dog-faced boy disappeared. He seemed to be able to appear and disappear at will, and some say that the apparition, which was seen again last summer, is the ghost of Ashland's original dog-faced boy.

Haunted Houses
of
Jacksonville

Back in 1851 a couple of traders, James Cluggage and John Poole, stopped to rest their pack mules for a few days in the valley north of the Siskiyou Mountains, before moving on south to the gold fields around Yreka, California. As they rounded up their mules on the morning of their departure, they discovered gold in "Rich Gulch". They staked out claims and hurried on to Yreka to buy tools and provisions.

In Yreka, word spread that the traders were buying mining tools instead of selling them. When the men headed north to work their new claims, a few curious California miners followed them, and, by the spring of 1852, claims had been filed on nearly all of the land surrounding Rich Gulch.

James Cluggage filed a Donation Land Claim on the future site of Jacksonville, and chose to name the new community Table Rock. In 1852, Jackson County was separated from Umpqua County and Table Rock became Jacksonville, county seat of Jackson County.

For a while, Jacksonville was a wide-open town, its streets crowded with miners in town for whiskey, excitement and provisions--in that order. Gunfights and fistfights were common and tolerance for violence, if not for racial differences, was the order of the day in the Jacksonville courthouse. A white man, who shot and killed a Chinese miner, was fined $25 for "discharging a firearm in the city limits".

After the gold supply dwindled, Jacksonville prospered for a while as an agricultural center, but, in 1883, the railroad bypassed the little town, and its economy began to decline. In 1927 the county seat was moved to Medford and Jacksonville was, in a way, frozen in time, a town with an exciting past but not much of a future. Hard times came with the Great Depression of the 1930's, when many residents of Jacksonville survived by mining gold from their own back yards. So much backyard and basement mining was done in those years that a cross section of the land on which the town is built would look like a slice of Swiss cheese.

Today's Jacksonville is a quiet remnant of the old west. Designated a National Historic Monument, the old town looks much as it did in the days before the gold gave out and the county seat moved to Medford. It is easy to imagine, as you walk the gracious, tree-lined streets or window-shop the line of brick facades along California Street that you have stepped back in time, that, except for the occasional car, Jacksonville might have looked exactly this way a hundred or so years ago, when John Miller and Herman Helms walked these very streets.

The Herman Helms House

Little Herminne J.
dau of
H. & A. Helms
died
Dec. 6, 1868
1 yr. & 10 mos.

> Tombstone found in basement of
> Herman Helms House,
> Jacksonville, Oregon

Herman Helms was born in Germany in 1832. He made his way to San Francisco in 1853, and then, in 1856, to Jacksonville, where he spent the rest of his life. He and a partner named Wintgen opened a bar in the back of the Table Rock Bakery which became the Table Rock Saloon, an important gathering place for miners and community leaders in Jacksonville.

Augusta Englebrecht was born in Germany in 1839, and she, too, came to America in 1853. With her parents, she settled in Yreka, California, in 1856. On April 25, 1862, she came to Jacksonville, and, the very next day she married Herman Helms. On their wedding day, Herman carried his new bride over the threshold of the small house he had built on Oregon Street, just over a block from the Table Rock Saloon.

By 1868, when the smallpox epidemic ravaged Jacksonville's population, three children had been born to the couple. Herminne, the youngest, contracted the disease and died. Because the winter weather had made the road to the cemetery all but impassable and because all public gatherings, including funerals, had been canceled in order to counteract the epidemic, Herman buried his youngest daughter in front of the house on Oregon Street.

The next ten years saw five more children born

TRAGEDY STALKED the Herman Helms family.
From left: Bertha, died of smallpox at family residence in 1889, age 15; Emma, shot by Anna's husband
in 1907, age 31; Elizabeth;   Mrs. Helms, died at
family residence in 1911, age 72; Edward, died in
1921, age 56; Herman Helms, died at family residence
in 1899, age 67; Matilda, died of smallpox at family
residence just eight days after Bertha's death, in
1889, age 17; Amanda, died in 1923, age 54. Front
row, from left: Anna, wounded in attack that killed
Emma, died in 1939, age 61; Harry, died in 1959, age
78. Herminne also died of smallpox in the family residence, before this photograph was taken. Photo
courtesy of Southern Oregon Historical Society)

THE HERMAN HELMS HOUSE, where five members of the family died. The original house is the
small wing at the rear. The two story addition in
front was built in 1878, over the original site of the
grave of Herminne Helms. (Rainy Day Press Photo)

to Herman and Augusta, and, by 1878, the small
house Herman built for himself and his bride had become too small. That summer a handsome two-story
addition was built on the lawn in front of the original house.

Some say that Herminne's remains were moved
to the Jacksonville Cemetery in 1878. Others believe
that the addition was built over her grave and that
she is still buried in the basement of the Helms

125

house. I looked for her grave in the Jacksonville Cemetery but could not find it, and, though the name Helms appears many times on the list of graves carried by the cemetery's caretaker, Herminne's name is not there.

The summer of 1889 brought another epidemic to Jacksonville, and more tragedy to the Helms household. This time it was typhoid fever. Matilda, 17, and Bertha, 15, contracted the disease and died in one horrible week in mid-July.

In January, 1907, the last chapter in the tragedy of the ill-fated Helms girls was written. Anna and Emma were running the Ella Rooming House at 655 Washington Street in Portland. Anna was married to, and separated from, a bicycle mechanic named Fred Martin. Martin felt that Emma was a wedge driven into his marriage and was insanely jealous of her relationship with Anna.

On the morning of January 6, Emma and Anna were relaxing at the rooming house when Martin burst into their room. When the women tried to leave the room, Martin said, "Neither of you attempt to leave this room." He drew his revolver, shot Emma twice and, as Anna ran from the room, he shot once at her.

Martin's first shot killed Emma. The bullet intended for Anna, according to a newspaper account of the event, "struck her in the back of the head, inflicting a flesh wound. Screaming and bleeding profusely, (she) rushed out of the house and fell into the street." Martin followed her to the door and tried to get another shot at her, but his pistol misfired. Then, "Rushing into the cellar, Martin stuck the muzzle of the pistol into his mouth and fired the last bullet into the base of his brain."

Martin left two suicide notes, one of which read, in part: "I am going to attempt to have us both together forever. I hope they will, if my attempt is successful, at least allow us the privilege of being put side by side and Emma as far from us as possible, as she has put us both where we will soon be."

The house that Herman Helms built still stands today, much as it was when he and his large family lived there. The tombstone that once stood on the lawn over the grave of Herminne Helms was, for many years, in the basement, under the addition that Helms built in the summer of 1878. When I visited the house in 1979, the tombstone stood near the fireplace in the comfortable front room of the old house.

In Jacksonville, whenever the topic of haunted houses comes up, the Helms house is among the first mentioned. The ghost of an old lady, it is said, sometimes, cries at night as she walks the hallway. Some say the ghost of a little girl, too, walks the hallway, or sits, crying, at the bottom of the staircase.

The John Miller House

John Miller was born in Bavaria, Germany, in 1830. He emigrated to the United States in 1850, settling first in New Jersey and then in Iowa. Shortly after his arrival in America he married Mary Smutz, who had immigrated to the U. S. from Baden, Germany. In 1860 they crossed the plains and settled in Jacksonville, Oregon.

Miller was a frontier gunsmith. He assembled gun parts, made guns, and stocked, in his Hunters' Emporium, all the weaponry necessary for successful frontier living. Thanks to the abundance of wild game and dangerous Indians around Jacksonville, his business was immediately profitable. He also owned and operated a hydraulic mining operation on the south fork of Jackson Creek.

By 1868, the Miller family had grown to include eight children, and the Miller house, big enough to house them all, was built on East Main Street.

The Miller children grew up and moved away, John and Mary Miller grew old and died, and the Miller house passed through a succession of owners,

127

GUNSMITH JOHN MILLER'S HOUSE doesn't look like this any more, but, around Jacksonville, folks believe that the old house, which was rebuilt in a considerably different fashion after a fire destroyed the upper floors, is haunted. (Photo Courtesy of Southern Oregon Historical Society)

one of whom--and this is where the tale of the ghost of the Miller House becomes confusing--was a gambler, a money-lender, or a debtor. According to various tales floating around Jacksonville, this owner was lynched one night because he was caught cheating at cards, hanged himself on the front porch, was shot by robbers, or shot himself. All agree that the body was found in the house, though some say it was dangling from a noose on the front porch an others believe it was found in an upstairs bedroom.

Whatever the means, the result is a ghost in the rebuilt Miller House. Doors open and close when no one is there, and footsteps are heard in empty hallways. A former resident of the house woke one night to find "a white figure" sitting on the edge of his bed. "Nothing frightening," he assured me--just another benign presence in the old mining town.

The Ghost
of
Grizzly Gulch

Some say that the Ghost of Grizzly Gulch was responsible for the disappearance of a miner in the mountains near Kirby (Josephine County) in the early part of this century. Searchers followed the miner's footprints through fresh snow into the mountains, where, in the middle of a clearing, they simply stopped. The miner was never seen again.

Applegate House

I drove out to the Applegate house on one of those September afternoons when the sky was so blue, the air so clean and delicious, the world so beautiful and pure it would break your heart. The sun--the early fall slanting sun that feels so good on your back in the cool afternoon air--played delectably with the furrows and fence posts and cattle in the fields, and it emphasized with shadows the shapes and softness of a landscape in the midst of a subtle turn from summer's deep green to the gorgeous reds and yellows of an Oregon autumn.

The Applegate house is nestled at the bottom of a hill a little to the north and east of the town of

Yoncalla, at the very end of Applegate Road. It was built between 1852 and 1856 by Charles Applegate, who, with his brothers Lindsay and Jesse, came to Oregon from Missouri in 1843. It is built mostly of cedar, lumber milled by the Applegates in their own small sawmill.

Charles and his wife Melinda had 15 children, and this house was big enough for them all. Its patch of grassy lawn backs onto the soft, brushy curve of the hillside. From behind a row of huge trees--walnut trees, I think--whose branches sweep low toward the ground, it seems to stare, imperiously, from big windows sunk like eyes behind the pillars of double-decker front porches, across the flat, fertile bottom of the Yoncalla Valley.

Wherever I went, seeking ghosts in western Oregon, someone pointed me toward the Applegate house. "Positively," said the lady in the Jacksonville Museum. "It's haunted." This gracious, friendly-looking old house is probably the most famous of Oregon's haunted houses.

"Well, I'm not sure," said the caretaker, as he unlocked the gate and ushered me past the profusion of "Beware of the Dog" and "Keep Out" signs. "One fellow was in there by himself and he picked up an old straight razor that was laying on the mantle. Something kept tapping him on the shoulder, like he wasn't supposed to handle that straight razor. He put it right down and came out of there mighty quick." We walked around to the front of the house. "But," he said thoughtfully, "I've tried it. I've picked up that razor plenty of times and nothing's ever tapped me on the shoulder. I just don't know."

Shannon and Susan Applegate, cousins and great-great granddaughters of Charles Applegate, and Shannon's children, lived in the old house for a while in 1971. Shannon wrote of their experiences with the Applegate ghosts in the spring, 1976 edition of **Northwest Review.** They heard thumps, voices, footsteps, the swish of long skirts in empty hallways and empty rooms. Occasionally, they caught glimpses of people who weren't there. They once hired a babysitter while they went to Eugene for an evening. When they returned, the babysitter, scared by the noises, had called "the lady from 'down the road'" to sit with her. "We had some tea and discussed possible explanations such as rats, wind, temperature changes, the old oil stove, etc." Shannon says. "We were no more convinced than the babysitter had been...especially when we heard the steady tread of of footsteps overhead."

The following story was published in the **Eugene Register Guard** on, appropriately, Hallowe'en, 1975.

VIBRATIONS

Quavering echoes of the dead still live on, some say, in creaky old Applegate House

By Dean Baker

YONCALLA--Shannon Applegate Mueller sometimes felt as if her mind was about to snap as she listened to a man and a woman arguing upstairs in her cold, dark, three-story house.

She knew no one was up there.

Alone except for her two small children, Shannon was terrified on those October nights four years ago. One evening she would laugh away the voices while talking long-distance to friends and family.

But the next night the voices would return, leaving her cringing in one of the creaking old house's five upstairs bedrooms, trying to drive them from her mind.

It didn't work.

"I thought I was being fanciful," she says simply. But the voices were easily heard in the noisy old house--even over the banging of the oil furnace, the groaning of the old floor joists, the whining of the wind and the rattling of walnuts being rolled between the rafters by energetic squirrels.

131

The voices couldn't be ignored. Shannon came to believe they were part of some unseen force trying to drive her from the 120-year-old house her great-great-grandfather Charles Applegate built. She decided to fight back.

"One night in my bedroom when the voices were particularly loud and I felt like I was about at the end of my rope, I decided to take the direct approach," she recalls.

Out loud she spoke into the darkness, proclaiming that she had as much right as any other member of the family to live in the house. Furthermore, she told the darkness, it was her intention to write an accurate history of the Applegate family.

She had been reading by kerosene lamp at the time, trying to catch the feeling of Oregon pioneer days, she says. When she finished the speech, she says, "The kerosene lamp dimmed. It was like a shadow passing over it and, sitting upright in bed, I fell into one of the deepest sleeps I have ever had."

That was in 1971. Today Shannon tells jokes about her visions, but she also believes her ears when she hears things in the house--or sees or smells them.

The voices she heard those first days were really there, she insists.

No, they weren't ghosts, she says. "It's not spirits coming back to haunt us. It isn't entities or individuals coming back to give us a bad time. It's literally as though the vibrations of former occupants of the house were caught in the walls themselves."

People who stay in the Applegate house have heard babies crying in the attic when there were no babies, smelled pipe smoke when no one was smoking, seen unoccupied chairs rock, heard broken clocks strike and fiddles and banjos play when no one was playing, seen silent womanly forms drifting through the house dressed in white, watched the whispy figure of a man in baggy pants.

And just this past week, they saw what seemed for an instant to be a person coming up the walkway. He vanished.

132

The house certainly has an air of antiquity. Shannon keeps its two front living rooms--the men's side and the women's side--filled with artifacts: pioneer furniture, fading photos of ancestors, old paint-

THE APPLEGATE HOUSE, near Yoncalla, is probably Oregon's most famous haunted house. Built between 1852 and 1856 by Charles Applegate, the Applegate house has been placed on the National Register of Historic Places. (Rainy Day Press Photo)

ings, rugs, books, lanterns, mirrors, clocks, Indian feathers, muzzle-loading rifles, elk racks, even a wheelchair belonging to a crippled forebear.

It is Shannon's ambition to write a history of

133

the 1843 pioneer migration in the United States, using her great-great-grandfather and his brothers
Lindsay and Jesse as a focal point. She has spent the
past five years working on the project and getting
close to her ancestors--sometimes too close, she wry-
ly admits.

"I am sure there are a lot of people who would
think I'm flamin' bananas," says Shannon.

And the 31-year-old Applegate heir readily admits to being a romantic.

"In an unusual way, I am in contact with the
past," she says. "I've made it my business to be.
These people who lived here have died, but they've
never been dead to me. I write about them. I make
them alive."

But Shannon insists there is more than her imagination propelling the whispy presences through the
old house. Friends and relatives have seen and heard
things, too, she points out. Shannon's husband Paul
confirms it. It's not unusual to hear knocking at one
of the house's four outside doors in the night, to
open the door and to find no one there, he says.

Even a babysitter was unsettled by eerie noises
much like those Shannon's great uncle Vince used to
attribute to "The Winter Ghost", a presence that
would take 12 or 13 steps through the attic and then
stop, leaving listeners waiting for the next step that
never came.

Some overnight visitors have been so frightened
that they vowed not to come back. Shannon's sister
Lisha was terrified by the sight of a woman in white
on the balcony.

Shannon's 30-year-old cousin Susan (also a
great-great-granddaughter of Charles) lived in the
house with Shannon for two years and had experiences similar to Shannon's--seeing whispy figures,
hearing voices and even on one occasion feeling that
she was silently communicating with the figure of a
woman.

So what is happening in the Applegate house?
Shannon has an explanation.

134

"First of all," she says, "I don't go along with the theory that there are spirits who have done something wrong and who must now walk abroad in unrest on All Hallow's Eve.

"But if somebody walks in and out of the same door and slams the screen 900 times in a lifetime or sits in a certain place on the porch, something may linger there--some energy," she says.

"Sometimes I think it's like a change in the wind current when you feel these things. Suddenly, because the wind is coming from another direction, you can hear sounds from away far off. They are maybe always going on--everything existing at once--and what you hear then is echoes.

"I don't think about them as ghosts or spirits. I just think that I am experiencing residues of very old energy. Some of it comes from specific people. Now, we can quibble about whether the past does extend into the present in this way," she says, "but I honestly accept it as a matter of course."

Most of the presences are just traces of sound and light lingering in the atmosphere, she theorizes. But sometimes the sense of the past is particularly strong.

Once Shannon saw an empty chair rocking and smelled pipe smoke and whisky at the same time. "In that case I really did feel that it was great-great-grandfather Charles," she says. "I believe that unequivocably. I even said, 'Hello'." She smiles at that memory.

The Applegate presences are real, she says.

At Yoncalla, human imagination and concentration--and perhaps even a dash of the occult--have gotten together in an antique house to make history come alive.

The Ghost
of
George Harding

Some say that the ghost in the theatre building at Western Oregon College is that of George Harding, the first theatre professor at the school. The theatre was originally housed in an old gymnasium and, some say, was haunted by the ghost of a former janitor. The old gym was torn down. When the new theatre was built, the ghost of George Harding moved in. He can be heard, walking--heel-and-toe, heel-and-toe--across the empty stage, and he has been known to sabotage lighting and other special effects a time or two, but, theatre professors and students at WOC know that if you talk to George he won't spook you.

The Ghost
in
South Eugene High School
Auditorium

Back about 1957, Robert Granke, a student in a stagecraft class at South Eugene High School, fell from a catwalk near the ceiling in the school's cavernous auditorium. Granke crashed into the seats far below and died from the impact of his fall.

Since that time, the story goes, those who sit in the seat in which Granke died will feel a hostile.

chilling, "presence", as though they were sharing the seat with someone or something not quite percept-able, at least in the ordinary manner of perceiving things. A brick once fell into the same seat, just be-fore its intended occupant sat down. Clearly, as the following story--first published in the **Eugene Regis-ter Guard,** October 27, 1974--attests, there is some-thing strange about the South Eugene High School auditorium.

Is somebody up there?
By Mike O'Brien

Up above the ceiling of the South Eugene High School auditorium, between the ceiling and roof, is a huge space full of scarred and ancient exposed beams, treacherous little catwalks that creak, narrow little corridors and low passages.

And through that space--along those beams, cat-walks, corridors and passages--moves somebody. Or something.

A manifestation. A presence. An indefinable thing. All right, let's say it flatly:

A ghost.

Whatever it is, it doesn't confine itself to the above-the ceiling area. It's been seen, felt and ex-perienced elsewhere in the huge auditorium by e-nough people that few would consider spending a night alone in the empty, echoing building.

Whoever or whatever it is apparently had made the auditorium its uneasy home since some time in the early 1970s. Some of the most chilling tales a-bout it come from David Nale, who's been South's drama director for about three years.

Nale's a rational sort who--along with others who've experienced the being--can put forth a num-ber of pragmatic explanations for the sinister things he's seen or heard or heard about.

137

The unexplainable

But none of these people seem completely or even partially satisfied with their own explanations. Others don't even try to find any.

One of the latter is Maxine Nielsen Walton, who graduated from South Eugene last spring.

"It's a feeling you get when you're working there, that somebody is with you, something is watching you," she says, with an edge to her voice. "And I don't think it's a friendly presence."

Nale claims to have no opinion about what the thing may or may not be. He does agree, however, to "deal in speculation".

And then he gets down to cases:

"Many people aren't aware of the huge space between the ceiling of the auditorium and the roof itself. "What I worry about as a faculty member is unauthorized people getting into an area where they're not supposed to be, so whenever there's a noise up there, I have to go up and look. If I had a dollar for every time I've gone up there after a noise I've heard, I'd be able to retire by now."

The space might have been designed by a madman. The way up is by ladders nailed to the walls, through queerly-shaped trapdoors and along narrow, dusty corridors. The area itself is so broken up into odd, unpredictable little spaces that it's difficult to know when you've arrived there.

It's dark, of course, and even when the lights up there are on, there are some shadows that won't be banished.

Anything may peer

Eeriest of all are the little openings from which a person--or anything--may peer out undetected and watch everything that goes on in the auditorium below.

It is up in that rabbit-warren that Nale has to go whenever he hears a noise.

138

But he has never found anyone up there. This despite doors and trapdoors with special locks, despite sending several people up different ladders, despite staking other people out at the bottoms of ladders, and despite conducting thorough searches.

Once, though, he thought he'd found something.

Nale was investigating one of the many noises but when he got to the area above the ceiling, he found that somebody down below had forgotten to turn on the lights up there. He knows his way around that area, so he plunged ahead.

"Then I saw what I thought was somebody wearing a white shirt," he says, "and I thought, 'Aha, I've got somebody this time.' So I followed this thing--I could just barely see this kind of glow--and I was following right behind it in the dark. I thought it went through a door. But when I followed--I walked right into the wall. When the lights came on, I saw I was a good ten feet from any door."

Many 'manifestations'

Nale says, without visible emotion, that "manifestations" of varying kinds have happened "at some time during every show I've directed here."

He has taken a number of precautions, including installing more trapdoors, putting heavy iron bars on conventional doors and buying some special locks.

None has worked.

"You can still hear something moving around up there," he says.

Mrs. Walton tells of stage properties disappearing during rehearsals for "The Bad Seed"--a play about innate evil--in 1972 and of people seeing something in the back of the auditorium. But far more chilling was an experience she herself had when she was an assistant director for "Man of La Mancha" at South last spring:

"When you're assistant director, you have to wait for everyone else to leave. Then you have to lock up. I was doing that one night when I looked up in the balcony where there's a walkway through the seats. There was something blue up there. It was elusive, but it was a blue-type figure up there in the balcony. I just froze, then I went and got the director (Nale). But by the time we got back..." her voice trails off.

This thing that scares so many people so often and so unexplainabley, makes itself known during the summer, too, if Vikki DeGaa's experience is any indication.

Early one afternoon

She and another woman were running the light board for the summer musical "West Side Story" in 1973. They arrived at the auditorium early one afternoon--5 or 5:30--to check out the light cues.

"You have to make the place completely dark to do that," Miss DeGaa says, "and then bring each light up individually." It's easy enough to make the auditorium completely dark since it has not a single window anywhere in it.

The two women were by themselves in the building, with Miss DeGaa standing alone on the dark stage and the other woman bringing up the lights one at a time. "And then," says Miss DeGaa, "I started hearing footsteps...very distinct and very deliberate."

When she says that, it is impossible not to think of the loose, creaking planks in the huge, echoing upstairs area. The footsteps Miss DeGaa heard started in the ceiling at the back of the auditorium, she says, and came progressively closer.

"At first I couldn't quite bring myself to look up there, but the footsteps kept coming closer so I looked up into the openings in the ceiling at the back part of the house and I saw these things that could've been legs passing in front of the opening, then they disappeared.

"Then, even though we couldn't see them any more, we both heard the footsteps coming closer and closer. So we dropped everything and ran."

140

Now, more than a year later, Miss DeGaa's eyes get large when she talks about it. So do others'.

Jeff Arnold's do when he describes an inexplicable and frequently-recurring manifestation of the thing. Arnold, who graduated from South in 1973, first mentions the almost standard "funny noises that have no cause or reason." He figures he experienced them nine or ten different times. Then he talks about visible aspects of the thing:

There's just no way

"You walk onto the stage and flick on the lights, then you see somebody sitting up in the balcony or standing behind the back row on the first floor. That's happened a lot. The thing is, there's no way anybody could get in without a key, and there's no way anybody could get out. But nobody's ever been found."

There are a great many other stories about what is or isn't in South's auditorium--stories about complex lighting systems being disrupted and drums being tampered with though the building has been locked all day and stories about people's names being called by an eerie voice.

And one melodramatic story about a brick falling from the ceiling--that's especially disturbing, since the auditorium is a wooden structure. There is simply no reason, except possibly a malevolent one, for any bricks being there at all.

But to really get the feel of how shattering an experience with this phenomenon can be, imagine yourself in Paul Martin's place.

Summer of '72

The time is the summer of 1972, and Martin, a theater technician, is working on the set for the Lane County Auditorium Association musical production, "1776".

As frequently happens when you get involved in

141

a show, you stay particularly late one night, long after everybody else in the crew has left.

All alone in that huge building, you keep fiddling with one particular effect on the set until, finally, in the cold, still hours of very early morning, you get it the way you want it.

Pleased with your success, smiling, perhaps even whistling or humming, you leave the stage--as Martin did--the hard heels of your shoes setting up little echoes as you walk out into the auditorium.

You sink into one of the soft red seats about midway back in the building. You settle back, basking in the solitude--totally alone.

Then the lights go out.

The Conser Lake Monster

I remember the first time I saw Albany.

Sleeping, southbound on I-5 on a chartered Greyhound, a truly awful smell invaded the bus and I awoke in a hail of accusations and denials as my team-mates tried to fix the source of this misery.

Out in the dark at the edge of the road, illuminated by bare lightbulbs that hung from wires high above the roadway, was a mine or factory or prison. I'd never seen anything like this. I wiped the condensation from the bus window so I could see more clearly. A large metal building and perhaps a couple of smaller ones, rectangular and gray and ugly, squatted in the middle. Radiating from them, like the ribs of a huge spider web, conveyor belts and augurs stalked on long, thin legs across great heaps of debris--talings, perhaps, from the mine. Steam, or smoke, plumed into the fall night from a dozen different sources, vents for some awful subterranean heat. In this whole wasteland not one human was visible.

142

The bus pushed on toward Medford. "Albany," someone said.

"Oregon?" I asked.

That was back in 1958. Now I know that the talings were wood chips, the machinery and buildings a pulp mill, and that there's more to Albany than a bad smell and hellish scenery. But, if the Conser Lake Monster had risen from the wood chips and waved as our bus passed that night, I'd have thought that he probably belonged right there.

During mint harvest in the summer of 1959, a graveyard shift truck driver was frightened half out of his wits by a tall, shaggy creature who appeared beside his truck on an isolated country road near Conser Lake, just a few miles northwest of the pulp mill. The creature loped down the road, peering into the driver's side window, and stayed alongside the truck with apparent ease at speeds up to 35 miles per hour. The creature became known as the Conser Lake Monster.

Not much attention was paid to the Conser Lake Monster when he first appeared, but when he turned up again the following summer, monster hunters came to the lake by the carload, and the brush around Conser Lake fairly bristled with shotguns and rifles.

The following stories appeared on the front page of **Greater Oregon,** Albany's weekly newspaper, on August 5 and 12, 1960.

SHOT TAKEN AT
MONSTER ON LAKE
By Betty Westby

Despite the vigilance of Linn County officers under Sheriff George Miller and state police who have responded to excited summons, the seven-foot monster, believed to be humanoid in form, still roams the shores of Conser Lake, between Dever-Conner and Millersburg, only six and one-half miles from Albany.

The creature first appeared last year when it ran beside a mint truck traveling near Dever-Conner and did not stop its flight through the open fields until the truck neared the mint distillery. The shocked driver said that the "monster", which resembled a shaggy white gorilla, peered curiously into the cab as it ran beside it.

Last Sunday night, seven teen-agers from Albany received the fright of their lives when the creature appeared in the lanes of Conser Lake (road) where they were out for a moonlight stroll.

Those who glimpsed the unearthly creature were from 15 to 19 years of age. They were Jim Westby, 16; Marilyn Simard, 15; Danny Everetts, 17; Ted Swarm, 16; Bob Swarm, 19; George Hess, 16, and Dick Marrs, 18.

Two of the boys had been lurking in the lane in order to jump out and startle their friends when they heard a crashing noise that they said was too large for a human source to cause. A seven-foot creature,

144

white in the moonlight, its features indistinguishable, came squishing down the lane, making a noise said one boy, as though he had water in his overshoes. The youngsters could not distinguish any garments, however, and described the same furry appearance of which the mint truck driver had told in his first encounter.

The two frightened boys ran screaming toward their friends, with the monster in hot pursuit. The boys, knowing they could not out-distance the creature, hid in the thick brush that surrounds the waters of Conser Lake.

Then the creature ran past the rest of the young people, in a blur, they said. It appeared enormous in the dark of the night, and when they turned their flashlights on it, it loomed huge above them. Many persons who have seen it say it is more than seven feet high and could weigh some 400 pounds. Some describe (it) as resembling "a big, white polar bear" while others cling to the theory that it is "something like a gorilla." But the teenagers who saw it on that night of horror, said it was "like nothing in this world" as it sped past them uttering a weird resonant cry which they described as "Fleep! Fleeoweep!"

While George Hess made his shaken report to Sheriff Miller, the other boys returned to summon reinforcements from older brothers and fathers. The creature appeared again that night, standing by a tree.

When the story broke over radio KGAL, Albany, this Tuesday, volunteer posses of teen-agers rendered the woods horrible as they fired at random at every bush. Last Saturday there were 200 persons of all ages in the gloomy Conser Lake area before 10:30. Cameras began to appear, and on the lower part of the lake, near an open meadow, Robert Ingram, 19, and two friends, shot a flash picture of some tall white creature on the opposite bank of the lake. Ingram said it straightened to what seemed more than seven feet, and fled into the impenitrable

(sic) undergrowth. The picture is in possession of
KGAL studios at this time, but if it proves to be
a picture of the mysterious creature of Conser Lake,
we hope to be able to publish it.

Your reporter, Betty Westby, approached the
Conser Lake area Sunday morning at the wee small
hour of 3:30 with five friends. We were the only
people in the area, and were armed only with a
camera and a flashlight. From the black waters of
Conser Lake we heard the hesitant croak of frogs,
which are said to halt their racket when the creature
walks abroad.

The woods were very still for about an hour as
we combed through the lanes and investigated several
large white snags and pale bushes. Then we had a
strange feeling that we were being watched, and my
friend, Jeanne Wattenberger, confirmed my feeling
that something was crouched on the hillside. Several
of the party scurried for the protection of the family
car, and the slamming of the doors may have startled
the watcher on the hill. We heard a tremendous
crashing in the brush and heard it rustling on the
ridge as a large form hurtled by toward the upper
end of the lake.

We hurried toward the source of the sound, but
the rustlings had stopped. Then, as the mists rose
smokily from the black, silent lake where the
creature at bay may have concealed itself, we heard
distant voices. In the dim light of dawn we
recognized Laverne Wolfe, 18, a husky young man
who was carrying a weapon. The barrel glinted in the
beams of our flash.

Wolfe told us that the monster must have
passed between our two parties, and that he could
show us footprints of the monster. The path came at
an angle down the hillside and across the lane
leading to the lake. The heavy impressions of a
great, spraddling foot, similar to a wedge or duck
foot, were six and seven feet apart. The young man
showed us with his light where the creature had

apparently rested. The impression of a large, heavy body had smashed the evergreen briars. Then it apparently leaped upright over seven-foot bushes, landing heavily more than seven feet away. We feared to penetrate the tangled briars for the fleeing creature may have been waiting for us.

"We feared to penetrate the tangled briars, for the fleeing creature may have been waiting for us."

We photographed the two sections of path and walked in the footsteps of the monster. We wear a size 8, but our footprint was lost in the three-foot wide impression left by the strange creature of Conser Lake.

Just a few hours before our arrival, 11:30 Saturday night, the monster may have been wounded. Mike Potter, 17, a husky red-headed Albany youth, armed with a .30-.30 rifle, was at the lower end of the lake area, where a small creek flows from the slough. He saw a large white form crouched by a heavy bush. It raised upright to more than seven feet, Potter said, and then crouched down again. When it reared up the second time he was ready and

147

fired at it. The creature spun part way around as though it had been struck in the shoulder. Potter and his friends took to their heels.

When they returned with state police, they found the area heavily trampled where the monster had first stood, and the brush was mashed down with the power of a steam roller's passage.

Officers in pursuit of the creature have had two hound-dogs literally torn to ribbons. On Sunday, two lads fishing in the broad afternoon sunlight at Conser Lake were startled by the appearance of the white creature and had to be hospitalized for shock.

Whatever it is, it has set all Linn County in a fever of excitement and has roused disgusted officers from their beds at ungodly hours.

DON'T SHOOT AT
MYSTERY MONSTER
OF CONSER LAKE

By Betty Westby
Guest Writer

The hue and cry after the famous creature of Conser Lake had died down a little, but we regret to say that the publication of the article has freshened the interest of a fresh group of Robin Hoods, coming from as far as Portland and Eugene in quest of the hunted humanoid.

True, he is large and frightening in appearance, but the actual fact is that he seems to be more curious than dangerous. The creature, which stands on two webbed feet, towers seven or eight feet, and his shaggy white hair has caused spectators to say that he resembles a gorilla. Others have likened him to a bear. Yet he is able to run upright for long distances, and has been known to keep pace with a frightened truck driver at the rate of 35 miles an hour.

Strangely enough, though he has encountered many human beings who were unable to protect themselves, he has offered no harm to anyone. Even the

small boys who were startled by his sudden appearance on the banks where they were fishing suffered
only from shock. The damage done in the killing of
the dogs was the natural reaction of a creature at
bay. If we found ourselves on a strange planet, or in
a foreign country, with every hand turned against us,
we would flee when pursued, and fight when corner-
ed.

If this is an extraterrestial creature from some
star beyond our ken, another form of life correspond-
ing to homo sapiens, then we do ill to turn a hostile
face toward it.

Now we will tell you an extraordinary tale,
which you may believe or not, just as you prefer.
This is the way it was told to us in all sincerity by
a local telepath. A telepath, as you may know, is
able to converse mentally with others, and has no
need for speech in understanding others. Some may
call such a person a mind reader.

"He doesn't like to be called a monster," she
explained to me as we listened in the still dark
woods of Conser Lake. "I shall ask him what he
would rather be called."

A little later she said, "Visitor or alien." When
I asked her if he objected to the word "creature"
(which I shall use hereafter) she said that he liked it
much better than "monster".

"He knows that we do not have a gun, but
there are others coming with a gun and he has to run
now."

"No, wait!" I said, my reporter's instinct fore-
most. "See if he will tell you where he is from."

But we heard the pounding of heavy feet on
the ridge above. It was the sound of a single-pacer,
such as only a biped could produce. The brush crashed ominously as a dark form hurtled by above us in
the thick brush.

Eagerly we rushed forward to try to catch a
glimpse of our strange "visitor", but we heard the
footsteps fade away in the distance.

As we ran fearlessly down the moonless lane,

we heard the murmur of voices in the distance. We came upon a group of young people, and one boy was packing a rifle, just as the alien creature had "told" my telepathic friend.

He told us that he could show us the path the fugitive creature had taken toward the lake and pointed out the footprints with the six-foot spread and showed us where it had jumped seven feet high to clear a bramble bush.

We measured the duck-like footprints which were impressed deeply into the woodland soil. They were three feet across at the wider part. My friend held the flashlight to point at the prints while I took a flash picture on panchromatic film. The picture shown here (no picture was published with the story) is not too clear, due to poor lighting conditions, but the dark impression shows where the creature of Conser Lake stepped.

Later in the week my telepathic friend returned with her children to the sunlit woods. As she stood beside the car, she felt impelled to look up on the hillside and saw the two pointed cat-like ears and broad white furry forehead of the Conser Lake creature.

This is their conversation, as reported by my telepathic friend:

"Is that you, Alien?"

"Yes, friend. I knew you would come back."

"Why don't you show yourself more plainly. I want to see you."

"Because your children would be too frightened, like the boys who were fishing by my water."

"But you didn't hurt them."

"I hurt no one. I mean no harm. I come with a feeling of interest, of affection for the creatures of earth."

"Yet everyone has chased you."

"I suppose I frighten them. Oh, why can't they leave me in peace?"

"I am sorry for you, alien friend. What are you called?"

150

"I am called Flix. There are many like me, but I am the one called Flix."

"That is a very funny name, Flix."

"It serves the purpose of identification."

"Where is it that you came from?"

The creature paused. "I am not sure you could understand. It is hard to put into earth terms."

"I am new at this telepathy."

"Yes. I can tell that. Very clumsy." The creature seemed amused at my little friend. "But I shall try to explain."

But they heard voices in the woods again, and another party of young people armed like a troop of guerrillas were trudging down the road.

The pointed white ears disappeared. His last message was, "They are chasing me again. I mean no harm. Goodbye, friend. Come back. I am lonely."

My friend's hazel eyes were bright with tears as she told of the plight of one alien against a planet of hostile people.

You may believe this or not. You may see it (as) a rare piece of fantasy or think we are "pulling your leg", but we know that telepaths have strange powers. Many persons have seen this creature in daylight and dark and have failed to identify it. The teenagers who first reported it to Sheriff George Miller said that it looked like "nothing on earth".

Freak of nature or alien from a world beyond, let's stop being trigger-happy and give the poor creature of Conser Lake a rest.

We urge parents to keep their boys and girls away from Conser Lake. It is a real wonder that someone has not been shot.

Boys with guns who are looking for a monster are apt to fire at a person through moving brush and kill some other boy or girl.

151

"I am called Flix. There are many like me, but I
am the one called Flix."

Conser Lake is hard to find these days. A narrow, murky, private slough, it sits in a brushy depression behind an old barn, three quarters of a mile
from the nearest public road. It cannot be seen from
the road, and no signs point in its direction.
Though its owner calls stories of the Conser
Lake Monster "garbage", it's not hard to imagine that
something strange might live here. From the old barn
a trail plunges toward the lake. It passes through

152

poison oak and high grass, over mouldering stumps and fallen tree trunks, past old machines, whose windows peer from the undergrowth like empty eye sockets. Snaggy trunks of broken trees pierce the low forest canopy. Shafts of sunlight dapple the undergrowth, but it is dark in here, and gloomy. The lake is narrow, the water, a thick, dirty brown, its surface broken where a log or stump waits like a crocodile. Listen! There are sounds--the crash of a branch, or something, falling into the brush, the splash of a fish, or something, on the water's surface, a low moan, like a far-off machine, or a cow or...a monster...

Index

Albany, Oregon 1
Alexander, Jim 6-10
Alpha-bit Cafe 4-5
Alvord Ranch 102
Anderson, Enoch 105-112
Angora Post Office 103
Applegate House 129-135
Applegate, Charles 130
Applegate, Melinda 130
Applegate, Shannon 130-135
Applegate, Susan 130-135
Arnold, Jeff 141
Ashland, Oregon 120-121
Astoria 80
Astoria, Oregon 67
Bailey, H. 119
Baker, Dean 131
Bakken, Lavola J. 114
Bandage Man 55-67
Battery Russell 67
Bayocean, Oregon 35-37
Bigfoot 54
Binford & Mort 47
Blackfoot Indians 90-96
Blue Mountains 80
Brewster, Bill 20-24
Butcher, Lawrence 45
Byars, William L. 119
Cannon Beach 55-67
Cape Foulweather 19
Cape Gregory 19
Cape Meares 35
Cape Perpetua 19
Chapin, H. L. 35
Christianson, C. 68
Clatsop Indians 40
Cluggage, James 121
Cockle, Dick 83

Columbia River 3, 45, 68-70
Conser Lake 142-153
Cook, Captain James 19
Coos Bay, Oregon 104
Cougar Creek 114
Cow Creek 116
Daily Astorian 69, 70
Daily Oregonian 68, 69, 70
DeGaa, Vicki 140-141
Devil's Lake 43
Devil's Punchbowl 23, 24
Douglas County 114
Enchanted Prairie 102-112
Everetts, Danny 144
Fish Lake 99-102
Fleetfoot, Chief 43
Flix 151
Florence, Oregon 3
Forest Grove, Oregon 70
Fort Stevens 67
Fortune, John 119
Frenchglen, Oregon 99
Fritz 100
Galesville Hotel 114
Gibbs, James A. 47-53
Gillespie, Major G. I. 45
Glendale, Oregon 120
Grande Ronde Valley 81
Granke, Robert 136
Greater Oregon
Griffith, Dr. Ty 82
Grizzly Gulch 129
Harding, George 136
Heceta Head 1, 3, 4
Heceta, Bruno 3
Helm, Mike 2
Helms, Herman, family
123-127

Hess, George 16
Horny Chessman 54
Hot Lake 79-89
Hyland, Geo. M. 36, 38
Indian Lake 43
Ingram, Robert 145
Irving, Washington 80
Jacksonville, Oregon 118, 121-129
Jefferson, Thomas 19
John Day Crossing 71
John Day River 71-72
Joseph, Chief 90-96
Joseph, Oregon 96
Klamath Lady 44
La Grande Observer 82
La Grande, Oregon 1, 81
Lake Erie 97
Laughing Devil Canyon 98
Ledyard, John 19
Leonard, Daniel 71
Leonard, Mary 71-72
Levens, Dan 116
Lewis and Clark Expedition 19
Lincoln County 43
Lincoln County Historical Society 19, 34
Linn County 144
Lithia Park 120
Louisiana Purchase 19
MacArthur, Lewis 102
MacClure, Evan 19-34
Mahane, Rick 74-78
Maloney, Mrs. Alice B. 102
Mann Lake Ranch 102
Mann, Irvin, Ranch 74
Mapleton, Oregon 4
Marrs, Dick 144
Martin, Paul 141-142
Mayo Clinic of the West 82

McAlder Homestead 113
Miller, George 144
Miller, John, family 127-128
Miller, Lischen M. 19, 28, 34
Moncton (ship) 20
Mueller, Shannon Applegate 131-135
Nale, David 137-140
Neahkahnie Mountain 39-42
Neal, John M. 69
Nehalem Indians 40
Nelson, David 74-78
Newport, Oregon 19
Nez Perce Indians 90-96
Northwest Magazine 35
O'Brien, Mike 137
Old Rocky 100-102
Opakahini, Lehui 20-22
Oregon Shakespearean Theatre 121
Owens, Richard 85-88
Pacific Coast Monthly 19, 34
Pattee, Dave 83-89
Pattee, Donna 83-89
Pendleton, Oregon 73, 74
Phy, Dr. W. T. 84
Pierce, Walter 80
Poole, John 121
Potter, Mike 147
Potter T. B. 35
Red Wolf 92-96
Reese, Bob 97
Rocky Mountains 20
Rogue River 104
Roseburg News-Review 114
Roseburg, Oregon 118
Rue 3-16
Sasquatch 54

155

Sea Lion Caves 4
Seaside, Oregon 54
Sexton Mountains 116
Siletz River 44
Siletz, Oregon 44
Simard, Marilyn 144
Siskiyou Mountains 116
Siuslaw River 17
Smith, Clifford 118
Smith, Florabelle 99-102
Smith, Harry 99-102
South Eugene High School 136-142
Spokesman Review 80
Steens Mountain 99-102
Stowelt, George 112
Straits of Anian 19
Surf, The 36
Swarm, Bob 144
Swarm, Ted 144
Tammen, Ann 5-16
Tammen, Harry 5-16
Tatone, Joe 96
Tillamook Head 45-53
Tillamook Indians 40
Tillamook Light 47-53
Tillamook Light 45-53
Tillamook Rock 45-53
Tillamook Spit 35
Tlesca 93-96
Trevenard, Zina 19-34
Trewavas, John R. 46

Two Good's Grave Creek House 118
Umatilla County Library 73-74
Union City Library 82
Union, Oregon 81
Van Vlake, Charlie 116-120
Van Vlake, Peggy 115-120
Waggoneer, George 90-96
Wahluna 92-96
Wallowa County 1
Wallowa County Chieftain 97
Wallowa Lake 1, 89-97
Walton, Maxine Nielsen 138
Wasco, Oregon 71
Welch, Harold 29-31
Westby, Betty 144, 148
Westby, Jim 144
Western Oregon College 136
Whale Rock (photo) 18
Whalers' Arms 20
Wheeler, H. S. 46
Wicklander, H. C. 96-97
Wiggins, Irene 89-90, 96
Wolfe, LaVerne 146
Yaquina Bay 20
Yaquina Bay Lifesaving Service 18
Yaquina Bay Lighthouse 19-34
Yaquina Head 20
Yoncalla, Oregon 129-135

156

The End.

Perhaps. . .

The Oregon Country Library

```
┌─────────────────────────────────────────────┐
   Conversations with Pioneer Women
  by Fred Lockley, compiled and edited by Mike Helm.
└─────────────────────────────────────────────┘
```

"These oral histories of Pacific Northwest women...are action-packed, adventurous love stories of our forebears who trudged to the Oregon Territory in the mid-1800s. This one is a diamond."
Los Angeles Times
"...an engaging, meaningful documentation of women's experiences on the frontier."
Seattle Post Intelligencer
"The trials of crossing the plains in a wagon and establishing a home in the Northwest wilderness are brought into sharp clarity."
Walla Walla Union Bulletin
"...of great use to history teachers, those who teach women's studies, and readers who enjoy the true flavor of frontier life."
Oregon Journal
"...a rare treasure..."
Corvallis Gazette-Times
"...riveting...a book to treasure."
Willamette Valley Observer

Conversations with Pioneer Women is recommended by *Booklist* and *Choice*, publications of the American Library Association. **Conversations with Pioneer Women** is a Small Press Book Club Selection. **Conversations with Pioneer Women** received the Pacific Northwest Booksellers Award for Literary Excellence.

"Yes, I like music, but when I was a girl the musical instruments we practiced on were the churn, the washtub, and the cradle. "
Mrs. Franklin Powell
Pioneer of 1851

"We started with two wagons and eight oxen. We got here with one wagon, drawn by an ox and a cow."

William M. Billyeau
Pioneer of 1852

Oregon's Ghosts and Monsters
by Mike Helm

"...familiar tales of regional phantoms and haunted buildings ...that sent shivers down the spine of at least one late-night reader."
Eugene Register Guard

"For readers fascinated by Oregon lore, this book will be hard to resist."

La Grande Observer

Tracking Down Coyote
by Mike Helm

"...a wonderful book. Helm...is a storyteller, historian, and writer of worth. His Coyote tales are delightful...
Sunday Oregonian

"...One of the best books of its kind I have ever read...Mike Helm is an excellent teller of tales and a fine hand at weaving experience, fact, legend and myth into an engrossing whole..."
Eugene Register Guard
Salem Statesman-Journal

"(Helm's) predecessors are Edward Abbey, Edward S. Curtis, John Muir, Henry Thoreau, W. P. Kinsella, with an echo of Carlos Castaneda...his scholarship approaches the religious...his best writing recreates journeys into the mind and legends of Coyote and his fellow Oregon deities, bringing ancient stories to life..."
San Francisco Chronicle

"Coyote would dig it."
What's Happening

A special offer for lovers of Pacific Northwest Literature

The Oregon Country Library discounted 10%.

Please send me:

____copies of **Conversations with Pioneer Women**, by Fred Lockley, compiled and edited by Mike Helm. 310 pages. ISBN 0-931742-08-0. $16.95 each.

$_____

____copies of **Conversations with Pioneer Men-- Bullwhackers, Muleskinners, Etc.**, by Fred Lockley, compiled and edited by Mike Helm. 358 pages. ISBN 0-931742-09-0. $17.95 each.

$_____

____copies of **Visionaries, Mountain Men & Empire Builders** by Fred Lockley, compiled and edited by Mike Helm. 300 pages. ISBN 0-931742-10-2.This book is presently out of print.

$_____

____copies of **A Bit of Verse: Poems (&Etc.) from the Lockley Files**, by Fred Lockley, compiled and edited by Mike Helm. 166 pages. ISBN 0-931742-13-7. $7.95 each.

$_____

____copies of **Oregon's Ghosts and Monsters**, by Mike Helm. 158 pages. ISBN 0-931742-03-X $9.95 each.

$_____

____copies of **Tracking Down Coyote**, by Mike Helm. 232 pages. ISBN 0-931742-16-1. $14.95 each.

$_____

Subtotal	$_____
less 10% discount	-$_____
Plus postage & handling	$_____
($1.20 for the first book,	
$.40 for each additional book)	
Total	
	$_____

Name_____

Address_____

City_____State_____Zip_____

NOTES

Mike Helm - 541-484-4626 - Eugene Oregon

NOTES

NOTES